PRAISE FOR
THE HERO'S JOURNEY

"In this seminal work, Dr. Andrew Dobo lays out convincing and practical steps that combine and advance EMDR frameworks within the power of myth. *The Hero's Journey* is what we all seek to understand and embrace. In this book, Andrew Dobo shows us how."

Laurie Beth Jones, internationally recognized best-selling author, speaker, coach, and trainer

"Dr. Dobo stands at the dawn of a new era of EMDR. He reads his clients with a kind of tribal savvy which he teaches to his students. He paves the way towards a new way to open the hidden depths of EMDR. You simply cannot put his book down. The information that he presents adheres to the soul. He brings a profound spirituality and inflamed passion that he holds towards EMDR to his readers, similar to the ten Sefirot of the mysticism of the Kabbalah which includes understanding, wisdom, power, love, beauty, splendor and healing."

Dr. Pamela Rinato, Licensed Psychologist
EMDRIA Approved Consultant

"When I first heard Dr. Dobo say 'Follow the client' I knew my experience as a counselor would be forever changed. In this book, *The Hero's Journey*, Dr. Dobo guides the newly trained to seasoned therapists by encouraging them to set themselves aside and let the unconscious do its work. I highly recommend *The Hero's Journey*. Expect it to challenge and inspire you to go outside the box as you hone your therapeutic skills."

Sandra B. Stanford, LMHC
EMDRIA Approved Consultant and Advanced Trainer

∽

"This book is amazing and so important. Dr. Dobo shares his discovery of his inner genius and teaches us how to discover our own. *The Hero's Journey* is a beautiful synthesis of modern science and timeless wisdom. Dr. Dobo provides us maps for both the wounded and the healer that bring what is sacred back to current psychotherapy. He challenges and then expands our current medical definition of healing, where 'success' is defined as simply symptoms lessening and shows actionable ways that lead to a deeper healing. A path to wholeness. This book is an invitation for any reader to embark on the most important journey we can ever take, the journey to find out who we really are meant to be."

Ryan Terry, LMHC
EMRIA Certified EMDR Therapist
Clinical Director at St. John's Recovery Place

∽

"Dr. Andrew Dobo's book takes us deep into the EMDR journey and introduces us to archetypes, dreams, and the language of the unconscious, so we can stop chasing the latest protocol and give our clients real transformational experiences with EMDR. A must-read for every EMDR therapist who wants to access their inner genius."

Rotem Brayer, M.Ed., LPC
EMRIA Approved EMDR Consultant and Advanced Trainer
Founder, The Art and Science of EMDR

⌁

"Dobo's book *The Hero's Journey: Integrating Jungian Psychology and EMDR Therapy* teaches us how to infuse the wisdom of Jungian Psychology into the robust healing power of EMDR Therapy, deepening our work in unimaginable ways. As I read through the chapters, I literally feel his heart and soul as he brings key points home through his real-life experiences of painful loss, synchronicity, and human love. This is a must read for so many reasons!"

Jackie Flynn, Ed.S., LMHC-S
EMDRA Approved Consultant and Advanced Trainer
Founder, EMDR & Play Therapy Integration Support

⌁

THE
HERO'S
JOURNEY

INTEGRATING JUNGIAN PSYCHOLOGY
AND EMDR THERAPY

DR. ANDREW J. DOBO

SOUL PSYCH PUBLISHERS

Melbourne, Florida

Published by

Soul Psych Publishers

1270 North Wickham Road Suite 16-602

Melbourne, Florida

Cover Design: Sky Diary Productions

Edited by Chris Kridler

Hardback ISBN: 978-0-9962207-6-7

Library of Congress Cataloging-in-publication Data Pending

CONTENTS

For my son Andrew R. Dobo, my hero.

Mythology was sacred to primitive people; it was as though their myths contained their very soul. The lives of primitive people were cradled within their mythology, and the death of their mythology, as happened with the American Indians, meant the destruction of their life and spirit.

John A. Sanford
in the book *He* by Robert A. Johnson

Most remarkable of all, however, are the revelations that have emerged from the mental clinic. The bold and truly epoch-making writings of the psychoanalyst are indispensable to the student of mythology; for, whatever may be thought of the derailed and sometimes contradictory interpretations of specific cases and problems, Freud, Jung, and their followers have demonstrated irrefutably that the logic, the heroes, and the deeds of myth survive into modern times.

Joseph Campbell
The Hero with A Thousand Faces

PROLOGUE

Mythology was sacred to primitive people. They understood that myths were not childish stories but rather that myth was part of their very soul. Jungian psychology subscribes to this idea. Jung saw the myth much like a dream. The dream is for the individual and the myth for all of humanity. The dream shows the individual psychological truths about themselves, and the myth reveals psychological truths about humanity as a whole.

This book aims to show the power of the standard EMDR protocol when administered by a skilled EMDR therapist who embraces the mythological pattern of the hero's journey in their work. We understand the standard protocol as the eight phases of EMDR therapy that Francine Shapiro developed in the late eighties and nineties. It is what we think of when we say EMDR therapy. By seeing these stages through the lens of the hero's journey and Jungian psychology, we unlock hidden secrets that allow for a deeper understanding of the client, their journey and the path that will lead them to healing.

Joseph Campbell dedicated his life to writing about the value of myth across cultures. George Lucas used Campbell's book *The Hero with a Thousand Faces* as a guide for his initial *Star Wars* trilogy. These films gave us our modern mythology and reminded us that we are all heroes in our own stories. These films touch us deeply because of their mythic nature, and they will continue to do so for generations to come.

In our exploration into the power of EMDR therapy, we will use Campbell's prescribed steps of the hero's journey as our therapeutic map. We will follow the archetypal transformation pattern that is activated during EMDR processing. The therapist must be aware of these mythic elements and understand how to recognize and utilize them. Once this awareness occurs, the therapist sets the hero's journey in motion. They will then accompany the client on this transformational journey toward wholeness.

We do not often think of therapy as a mythic adventure, but this book will awaken this rich, alternative way to think about EMDR therapy with our clients. EMDR can activate the client's heroic journey to their true self. The client moves through the same steps as the hero that Campbell describes.

My first book explained the six stages a client goes through during EMDR therapy as they go through a transformational process. These six stages are like gravity. They are a law, not a theory. My first book compared these stages to the Christian story of Christ's death and resurrection.

This book adds a new layer to the six stages of transformation. As it turns out, the twelve steps of the hero's journey outlined by Joseph Campbell occur within these six stages. So the steps in this EMDR process are shared in hundreds of myths, stories, plays, movies, and literature. If a drama does not follow this pattern, we do not like the movie, book, or whatever it is. This pattern is hardwired in our DNA and is ignited during the EMDR process. So the client is truly the hero in their life story, and we are their companion. This view adds a richness to the process, a richness that is lost in almost everything we do in our society. I hope you will take this journey as you learn to hold mythic space in an evidence-based, fast-paced world—the world that has lost its mythology.

When a new EMDR therapist comes to me for consultation, I am surprised at how little discernment is used when responding to a query. This lack of attention may be because Shapiro discourages repeating phrases the client says or emphasizing what they say. This perspective limits the power of EMDR, and this is one of those rare times I disagree with Shapiro. For the most part, I believe she has done more to reduce human suffering than anyone else in our modern world.

This new way of thinking does not take away anything from the standard protocol. So often, clinicians say the standard protocol is not working, so they look for some new protocol for some problem they cannot seem to solve. I have never needed a new protocol. Shapiro's standard protocol stands the test of time and has all the healing power a therapist will ever need.

In my experience consulting with EMDR therapists, their issue is not that the standard protocol is not working; instead, the trainee is missing 80 percent of EMDR's power that is occurring within the session. As I review my consultee's videos, without exception, they miss the most powerful statement and move along in some predetermined way. They do not follow the client, and when you do not follow the client, you are ignoring the unconscious, which wants to help with the healing process.

This loss of opportunity happens for two reasons. First, they have a preconceived plan of what to do during an EMDR session. Shapiro, as we will see, says never to do that, never have preconceived ideas of what you are going to do during the session. The client leads the therapist, not the other way around. Second, they do not understand or recognize the language of the unconscious, which is the most healing material that occurs during an EMDR session, thus the power that is right in front of the therapist is lost. This robust material is squandered.

This book explains which material that manifests during EMDR processing is of high value and which is not. We will discover what material is from the transcendent self that Jung talks about and what material is not. With this sophisticated understanding of the happenings during EMDR, the therapist will accelerate the client's transformation to their true self.

In his book *Between Heaven and Earth*, Robert Johnson shares what his teacher Fritz Kunkel, a Jungian analyst and writer, said was the best way to understand psychology. Kunkel said, "You should read Greek mythology, study Jungian psychology or wait and watch—waiting and watching is best." Kunkel would have mentioned learning EMDR, I am sure, but he died before it was discovered.

What exactly is the therapist watching and waiting for in this primarily silent process that is EMDR therapy? The client is listening for the language of the unconscious to speak. The problem is the unconscious has its own language. Sadly, few therapists are trained to recognize this language. Ironically, it is this very language that reveals the self-healing power of the human psyche that Shapiro and Jung both subscribe to in their therapeutic models.

Most therapists are dedicated to their work. Most spend a great deal of time and money seeking trainings to enhance their skills. This effort usually expands knowledge but does not always lead to improvement in their therapeutic skills. It is like a guitar player who wants to improve their skills as a musician. Rather than listening to themselves play to review their skill, they buy a new guitar and think it will make them a better musician. It does not make them a better musician. It might give them a few more options in terms of the sounds they can play, but they have the same ability, and that new guitar does nothing to improve their musical skill. Their craftsmanship is still the same.

This book combines all three of Kunkel's recommendations to improve the craftsmanship of the therapist in their practice of EMDR therapy. The craftmanship improves by understanding the power that exists in EMDR's standard protocol by simply waiting, watching, and listening with a new, extraordinary understanding of this unconscious language that C.G. Jung so clearly defined

Finally, the reader will see how myth is alive and well in the EMDR therapist's office. The reader will learn how Jungian understanding enhances the power of EMDR therapy.

Hopefully, you will give the logical left side of your brain a rest and join me in this hero's journey, where creativity and access to your inner genius are discovered and awakened. If you allow yourself this inner mythic discovery, let me say there is nothing like it. If you venture into this landscape, you will never look back, and all you have to do is wait, watch and listen.

Andrew J. Dobo
Melbourne, Florida
November 18, 2022

PART ONE

THE HERO'S JOURNEY WITHIN EMDR THERAPY

CHAPTER I

ACCESSING MYTH

HOLDING MYTHIC SPACE IN AN EVIDENCE-BASED WORLD

S ince this is a book about EMDR and myth, and myths are stories, let's begin with a story. Ryan is a consultee of mine. He and I are cut from the same cloth, although my cloth is much older, about thirty years older. When I work with advanced EMDR clinicians like Ryan, I teach them to stop doing whatever they are doing. Not that what they are doing is wrong, but the nature of this advanced way of working starts with "not doing." I try to get these trainees to stop thinking, assuming and ask them to "just be." Turn all thinking off and just wait, watch, and listen. They usually look at me like I have three heads, but not Ryan. He gets it.

Carlos Castaneda wrote a series of popular books in the 1970s and '80s. It was unclear whether they were true; he was a mysterious writer who avoided the press—another J.D. Salinger personality. One of the stories Castaneda shared in his book *The Teachings of Don Juan: A Yaqui Way of Knowledge* is relevant to our story.

Don Juan is Carlos's teacher. Don Juan told Carlos, "Today,

you must find your place of power." Don Juan continued his instruction, "There is a place on this porch that is your place of power, and only you can find it." Castaneda described the porch as significant because it almost surrounded the entire house. His teacher described this so-called place of power as the spot on the porch where Carlos would feel natural, happy, and safe.

Castaneda describes his frustration while searching for his place of power. After hours of struggle and frustration, and as the sun began to fall and the stars and moon arrived, after getting up and down, sitting and waiting to feel something dozens of times in this process, he became so tired that he gave up and fell asleep. He felt ashamed when he awoke the following day because he failed the task. Much to his surprise, Don Juan congratulated him for successfully finding his place of power. Don Juan said, "You have found the spot." [1]

Carlos succeeded by letting his guard down and by stopping his internal dialogue. He stopped trying, and in that moment of exhaustion, he allowed himself to "just be." He expressed his reality, "exhaustion," and found a comfortable place to fall asleep. In that moment of just being, he found his place of power. Within his sense of failure, he found success. Once he stopped trying and absorbed the present moment, he found his place of power. Therapists must know their place of power.

I'm not a yogi; I don't meditate very often. I don't do yoga. I don't burn sage. I eat too much, exercise too little, and age faster than I would like. But I have a place of power in my home and my office, and so do you.

When I am in my place of power, I am mono-focused. As I write these words, I am mono-focused. When I am in front of a patient, I am mono-focused. Therapists are fortunate. Johann Hari says in his book *Stolen Focus* that the average American worker is interrupted every three minutes, according to Professor

Gloria Mark at the Department of Informatics at the University of California, Irvine. The detrimental effect of these interruptions is enormous. The loss of brain power, deep thinking, and innovation is irretrievable, but that is a topic for another time.[2]

Therapists have the rare privilege of working in an uninterrupted environment. When a therapist's door is closed, there is a deep respect for the sanctity of the therapeutic hour. Anyone on the other side of that door, even the uninitiated, knows not to interrupt a therapy session. Therapists have an enormous opportunity to be mono-focused in the present moment without interruption. Sadly, few therapists take advantage of this rare situation where they can turn their brains off and just be. This book will hopefully change that reality.

I do not think or do anything when I am with a patient. At those moments, I don't even know my name. I am listening, watching, and waiting. I am waiting for it. What am I waiting for? Well, that's what this book is all about. It is about unlocking the mythic presence and the wondrous mystery of the healing power of the human psyche through EMDR. In these creative moments, the client has access to the self, the collective unconscious, and the inner, wiser, transcendent part we all possess—that part of our psyche that knows everything that has ever happened. Most therapists do not even know such a thing exists.

Now, in my sixties, the joy comes not only from my clients but also from those I am fortunate to train, my consultees, and dedicated therapists like Ryan. I try to teach them to hear the mystery and the magnificence of the unconscious. It's a new language. It's a secret language; only a few recognize it when they hear it.

This magic is a two-way street. It is not only expressed by the client and identified by the wise EMDR therapist, but the therapist is often immersed in their silent internal process. The superior EMDR therapist follows the client and does not lead the process. Again, a rare idea these days. The key is to encourage this sense of "not knowing" but trusting that the needed thing will show up at the perfect moment. The hard part is teaching the consultee to be patient, trust, and stop trying to make something happen. These are not revolutionary ideas. Shapiro warns of the overactive therapist in much of her writing, as we will see later.

When the therapist is fully present with the client, the inner genius is available to both the therapist and the client. Often in that darkest moment of confusion in a session, the stroke of genius will strike. When it does, it is like a lightning bolt of transformational power; everything changes in that unplanned electric moment of creativity. Accessing this inner genius cannot happen if you are talking or thinking. Any internal or external distraction destroys access to the creative moment. This inner genius occurs in the silence of flow. We will discuss "flow" shortly.

Ryan is a quick study. Unlike me, he does meditate; he also practices and teaches yoga. He can shut off his mind and listen. He has told me repeatedly, "Praying is talking to God, and meditation is listening to God." He is a student of being in the moment. Meditation is not the only way to learn how to be in the moment, although it might be the best way. I got my transcendental meditation mantra in 1972; I cut my teeth on "listening and waiting" as a musician.

I am a terrible musician, but terrible musicians can love music as much as enormously talented ones. For me, music wasn't about being a musician; music was about learning to learn. I did not know it at the time, but music taught me how to learn to concentrate on a problem for hours on end. It taught me what is required for creativity to occur. Music taught me when to play; this skill transferred to therapy. It taught me when to speak or not speak and when to think or not to think. Ryan has a natural ability to be, and the results of his work demonstrate this skill.

Ryan was in one of those sessions where something was happening, but something was missing. His client, whose wife passed away eighteen months earlier, had not yet cried about her death. His client was sad and expressed sadness with no tears. His client was not sure if he had ever cried about anything in his life. He said, "You know, Ryan, boys don't cry. That's what they told me as a kid." As the session was slowly ending, Ryan and his client were frustrated by the client's inability to cry. Creativity and self-healing require patience. The inner genius has no schedule. It cares nothing about time or space. It requires enormous discipline and patience, something sorely lacking in our world.

In EMDR, things work out best without intention. C.G. Jung knew this when he said, "Do you not yet know that the way to the truth is without intention?"[3]

So if there are no tears, then maybe there are not supposed to be tears. In this case, from some unknown place within, Ryan was "just being" with his client as time started to run out in the session. Without thinking, some strange thought came to him in a flash, and he blurted it out. He said, "You know, in Chinese medicine, they say that unexpressed grief is held in the lungs." This single out-of-the-blue, unplanned, mysterious "why the hell did I say that" statement caused an immediate eruption in his client. At that moment, his client glared directly at him, and he took in the deepest breath he ever saw a client take, a mythic breath from the heavens, and out came the loudest wailing sob he had ever heard, and this man sobbed a lifetime of grief in the next minutes of that session. The dam broke, and the client was on his way to a completely authentic expression of grief and transformation.

Although reluctantly, Ryan had put all the elements together for this mythic moment to occur and finally listened to his inner creative genius. Like Castaneda, he thought he had done something wrong. The Greeks call this a Kairos Moment, and in

Sanskrit, it is known as ksana, or "flash in time." Americans might call it a "stroke of genius." Ryan had an encounter with his inner creative self. These moments frequently happen for the masterful EMDR therapist. The more the therapist understands how to create the environment for this to occur, the more often it can be replicated.

If we examine what happened in Ryan's session, the client was "not knowing." *Why can't I cry? Do I have to cry? Should I try to cry? Is there something wrong with me because I can't cry?* Ryan is also in a similar state of "not knowing," asking himself these similar questions. With patience and trust, what was not known or understood a few minutes ago became understood. The answer was provided, not from books or knowledge but silence, self-healing, our recipe to create a mythic space for the inner genius to be heard.

Michael Meade tells us that people can prepare for this moment by studying and making careful plans. Still, the Kairos Moment only comes when you put aside all plans in favor of vision and inspiration.[4] Not only did Ryan heal his client, but he also created a new interweave for the entire EMDR therapy community. The Chinese medicine interweave is now available to use to break through stalled or resisted grief. An actual creative moment—a Kairos Moment. His inner genius emerged, and Ryan heard it, and, as we say in EMDR, he went with it, although reluctantly.

In our consultation, like Carlos Castaneda, Ryan was unsure what he did was right and thought he had failed because he did not use an "EMDR technique" from one of those EMDR books. I assured him that his *stroke of genius* was a thing of beauty. He stopped trying, stopped thinking, and just waited, watched, and listened. Suddenly, like a mythic lightning bolt, creativity struck, and like magic, there was the perfect statement delivered at the ideal moment for the struggling client. He encountered his inner genius. He heard its voice, listened to it, and provided the message. That moment of not knowing was a new creation for the world to use, at least the EMDR world. He just invented the Chinese medicine interweave. His stroke of genius, his Kairos Moment, and his ksana flash in time changed his client's world.

Everything Ryan had experienced in his life was available to him in the mythic space of waiting, watching, and listening. Then the perfect thing from some part of his life, the vastness of his psyche, from all of his units of human achievement amassed came the ideal words, delivered in the perfect moment to the perfect client that changed everything.

This book instructs therapists to replicate this phenomenon regularly and often. If Ryan had been thinking about an EMDR intervention or tried to chase the affect or any of the things he is trained to do, he would have shut off access to the wisdom within. That inner part of ourselves knows every word we have ever heard, read, or seen. It is all stored in our collective unconscious, which Jung described as a reservoir of images, usually called *primordial,* meaning "first" or "original." Humanity inherits these images from its ancestral past that includes all of the human spiritual heritage of mankind's evolution. Within this psychological structure are contained mythological motifs, images and archetypes waiting for us to access. But we must be solely focused on the client in front of us. We must put aside all agendas and plans and be completely present—watching, waiting, listening, and patiently trusting. Trust that what we need will emerge when we need it and realize everything we need is right in front of us.

CHAPTER 2

SETTING THE STAGE FOR THE HERO'S JOURNEY

THE THERAPIST'S RESPONSIBILITY

To create the mythic space, the therapist must possess certain qualities. Most of these qualities fly in the face of what therapists are taught in school. These qualities are necessary for any profession where creativity and troubleshooting are highly valued skills. When everything is said and done, the essence of EMDR therapy is a self-healing process. The therapist only intervenes if there is trouble.

The first quality for the therapist is to be able to put plans aside and just wait, watch, and listen. Usually, therapists are trained to be good listeners. Mythic listening is different. It is much more sophisticated than paraphrasing or reflecting a feeling. Like most mythic elements, there is a duality in the listening. Mythic listening is simple and complex simultaneously.

This advanced way to listen does not only refer to what the client says, but also care must be taken as it relates to the therapist's inner voice. The usual thinking, planning and self-talk that therapists engage in during therapy sessions must be turned off. All inner thinking and planning must cease. Only in silence can you hear the voice of the inner creative self. If Ryan was thinking about some preplanned intervention, he would never have had access to the unexpected idea of mentioning Chinese medicine as the key to his client's healing. This inner power reveals something that was unknown to both the therapist and client only minutes before he uttered those words. "Out of darkness, light," as the saying goes, hence the power of not knowing, but only by waiting, watching, and listening does the transforming power of myth appear.

Michael Meade calls this creative self that Ryan accessed *the inner genius* that resides within each of us. The problem is most of us do not know this part of ourselves. We usually do not believe we are geniuses, nor do we know how to access this inner power. Ironically, if by some chance this inner voice does speak to us, we do not recognize it or utilize it; we ignore it. This book is written in the service of changing that. This new way of thinking gives the therapist and the client permission to be creative, to break rules if there is a clinical reason to justify it.

There is a significant increase in problem-solving power when the therapist is not completely bound to rules, which unintentionally suffocate creativity, drastically limiting the healing power of EMDR. When the therapist has the freedom to use their experience, education, observation and life experience while working with a patient rather than being bound to rigid rules that make little or no sense, the inner creative genius is permitted to appear. The creation of this environment allows this creative energy to come alive within the client as well, although drawing from a different well of knowledge and experience. This creative access leads to innovation, healing, and discovery.

Let's continue as we develop a recipe for being perfectly present, which creates the environment for the creative moment. This method of therapy is an art and has much in common with artistic endeavors. Each one of us possesses our personal and unique creative self, but we are often so bogged down with intellectual endeavors that our creative energy is extinguished. This book is a reminder that our creative force is always there, waiting to be accessed. Let's take a look at how you can develop this healing power that lives within each of us.

THERAPIST'S QUALITIES: EDUCATION, PLANS, AND PREPARATION—KNOW THYSELF

Healing in psychotherapy comes from several sources. First, Carl Rogers and Eugene Genelin's research shows that the healing that ensues during psychotherapy comes from the client's internal experience. They also report that the healing of a client has little to do with the words spoken by the therapist or therapeutic techniques but rather with this internal *self-healing* power of the client's psyche.

John Sanford adds to this equation. He tells us that the internal effect on the client comes from two sources. For Sanford, the personality of the therapist is of high value. The personality hopefully develops rapport and trust that is exchanged between the client and the therapist. Second, he too agrees that the value of the client's internal experience provides self-healing power from the client's unconscious.[1] All three of these men reject the idea that technique or theory is the ultimate reason people heal. All three agree that the client must have an internal experience. All three of these men worked before the discovery of EMDR, so dreams were one of their primary sources of the internal experience. Now that we have EMDR, we know it always creates an experiential event and often a powerful internal experience. Shapiro also understood the power and necessity of the internal experience.

Let's discuss the therapist qualities necessary for creating the environment of not simply an internal experience but a mythic, numinous, and transformational experience. We want to develop skills so that this event does not just happen randomly but regularly and frequently. This can only happen if the therapist possesses the skill to create an environment for the transformational moment to occur.

Meade tells us that one must prepare for the Kairos Moment. The first part of the preparation is the therapist's education, a road all therapists know well. We begin our educational experience by attending a K-12 school system. This education system is a necessary first step. Within this often uninspired system, there is a pecking order that develops because of talents and interests. He's a jock; he excels at sports. She's a geek; she excels at computer science. He's a guitar player; he excels at music, and she loves to paint; she excels at art. Then some are lost in the middle, those of us who do not seem to excel at anything. This lack of identifying skills in students is the problem with traditional education. Children who rise to the top of their pecking order, the kids who know what they love, are the lucky ones and in the minority. No ten-year-old wakes up and says I want to be a trauma psychologist when I grow up.

For those who are not so lucky, perhaps Jung understood this reality when he said, and I'm paraphrasing, life really does begin at forty; up until then, you are just doing research. This decades-long search for purpose is true for most of us.

The journey to find our authentic purpose can be a somewhat mysterious process that only makes sense looking back on the journey after you have arrived at the destination. Robert A. Johnson, a Jungian analyst who wrote *Between Heaven and Earth*, examines his life events in the rearview mirror. He describes the enormous significance of seemingly random encounters, chance meetings, and physical struggles that brought him to his true purpose. He calls these events, each of which changed the course of his life, *slender threads.*[2] As we journey through this book, some of my slender threads will be shared. It is clear now but not at the time that many of these were extraordinarily mysterious, as you will see. Just for the record, I did not begin my journey to become a psychologist until I was forty years old. Jung was right. I needed forty years of research before my path became clear.

The therapist must know and understand themself. Therapists must do their own interior work. This requires deeper levels of revelation that come from accessing one's inner reality. To develop this, they must journal, attend to their dreams, and come to know themselves in a deep and profound way. It is essential that EMDR therapists seek out an EMDR therapist for themselves as part of this internal journey. We will discuss the nuts and bolts of this inner journey in part three of this book. We all have gifts that lead to a vastly wider capacity where we can reach greater heights in our authentic purpose. This internal work informs the external self so a better understanding of who you are out in the world becomes clearer.

Most of this discovery is within you, but a mentor or companion is also needed. We will discuss this a little later. You are the only one who can discover your life's purpose. Only you can define the goal and navigate the necessary steps toward your purpose. In this journey, you can guide your clients as they take on their adventure to their truth. It is along this journey that you will discover the genius within. Once there is a sense of that purpose, problems and obstacles fall away, or if they do occur, they never feel insurmountable. There is motivation and clarity once you know you are on your path.

This inner work is an artistic journey. We are talking about accessing the inner genius to access creativity. It brings forth the unexpected and powerful, just like Ryan's Chinese medicine inter-weave. Ryan's moment was all those things—creative, innovative, unexpected, powerfully transformational, numinous, and healing—all in a moment.

Why artistic? Pat Metheny, jazz guitarist, composer, and inno-vator, is a student of this process, or perhaps an *expert* of the process better describes him. He has literally been on this inner journey toward excellence and creativity for about forty-seven years. He journals daily and studies himself by examining what he does before and after a show and the time between shows. He identified one crucial factor that can be measured that is neces-sary for this mysterious creative environment to exist, fostering the opportunity for the creative moment to occur every night on the bandstand. He calls it "units of human achievement."

Pat trademarked this phrase. One of Pat's life's purposes is to figure out how his inner genius could be accessed every night. Metheny stated he achieves a high level of performance by under-standing what enhances or interferes with his playing. He, too, seeks his Kairos Moment in his improvisation and spent a lifetime studying why he played great last night but not tonight. What was the difference between those two nights?

He asked himself these questions every night for the last forty-seven years and examined variables within himself and factors outside himself to increase his chances of reaching excel-lence. He recently spoke at the Conference for the Society of Neuroscience and reported that he could access his inner genius consistently every night on the bandstand when he plays. At age sixty-seven, he stated he could get himself there most nights. He is not 100 percent but at least 85 percent. He said he had figured it out.[3]

Metheny's profound and consistent self-examination toward excellence is rarely done by therapists. Tools toward excellence, such as self-examination, are lacking in their education. It is rare for therapists to watch videos of their sessions with clients. Reviewing videos should be one of the bare necessities in the search for excellence. My consultees learn this quickly by simply watching themselves. Even without my feedback, they notice their mistakes. One of the critical factors of accessing inner genius is preparation and the search for excellence.

Therapists look at the therapeutic process through the lens of transference or countertransference. We will blame the lack of improvement by the client as resistance or denial or any other garden-variety defense mechanisms. These are all legitimate. If we watch a video of a resistant client, often there is a solution that is not apparent in the actual session. How can you get better at something if you don't go back and examine your work? Rarely do we look inward and ask ourselves, "Why were my sessions so effective yesterday but today they are not going well?"

Metheny has asked, "How can I be better?" practically every day of his life. He has searched for excellence in music. He leads by example and encourages anyone, no matter their job, to ask, "How can I be better today?" "Why was I so great yesterday, and today, not so much?" This seems like a simple question, and it is, but getting to the answer, well, that requires an in-depth look at oneself. Hopefully, you will consider the inner journey after reading these pages.

For Ryan, the inner genius showed up randomly and unex-pectedly. Through your inner work and expanding your units of human achievement, there will be consistent access to this power within. The inner genius awaits.

This idea of units of human achievement can be viewed in our example with Ryan. In his late thirties, Ryan has mastered several things in his life. He is an advanced meditator and yoga practi-tioner, as well as an instructor in those areas. He is a practicing martial artist. He is a skilled surfer and swimmer. He also played college football. He has an advanced degree and manages a group of drug and alcohol clinics, as well as sees clients. Ryan is also a father and a husband as well as a son.

Unfortunately, Metheny does not clearly define what he means by a single unit of human achievement. For our purposes, anything that takes years to accomplish that is considered an achievement by the person is a unit, and the more of those you have, the better therapist, musician, scientist, artist, firefighter or whatever it is you do, you will be. Ryan's units took years to master, and mastery requires focus, concentration, passion, effort, and time.

Now someone who is ten years Ryan's junior, who has spent their life in school without many other achievements, will have fewer units of human achievement. Some of the qualities needed to access the inner genius have not developed yet, but they will if the therapist takes on the inner work. Part III of this book will offer suggestions that foster inner genius access.

There are developmental stages in any art, including therapy. There is a struggle to learn the language and techniques. When your understanding builds and grows beyond the boundaries of your discipline, you have access to the possibility of innovation. Creativity is simply putting two things that already exist together in a new way. If all you ever do is read EMDR books, you will be a skilled EMDR therapist, perhaps, but you will be closed off from creativity and innovation of the inner self.

There are stages to achieving this level of mastery as an EMDR therapist. I remember struggling through these stages while learning jazz piano from one of Pittsburgh's most talented jazz musicians, Frank Cunimondo. Frank could be impatient, especially with someone like me who had modest talent—great desire but little talent. Frank was expressing his frustration with me during this lesson and yelled, "Andy, would you stop thinking and just play." He continued, "I can see you thinking. Stop thinking and just play." I was just in my early twenties, and although I had a degree in music, I was new to jazz. My units of human achievement were few.

I wasn't ready to just play. I was just learning the jazz alphabet, so thinking is part of the arduous process on the road to mastery. You can't paint a masterpiece if you don't even know how to hold a brush.

I can "just play" now, and like Castaneda, I realized I was able to "just play" unexpectedly. It was one of those days where you just sit down to mess around at the piano when you aren't thinking; you're just in the moment, letting whatever wants to come forth to come forth, and there it was. I wasn't thinking. I was just playing. It was like those hands were not my hands. I did not recognize them. So this is what Frank meant when he said, "Stop thinking and just play," a statement he made to me twenty years earlier when I was a kid. Now, here I am, a psychologist, and I can just play. I can just play in every EMDR session I perform. There is a process. EMDR was way easier for me than the piano ever was. What I learned while playing the piano helped me enormously as an EMDR therapist.

Metheny does a great job at discussing the process of education as a step to discovering your "thing," as he calls it, "your inner genius." Metheny talks about a jazz musician's education. The musician must know every song in the "Real Book" (an encyclopedia of songs every jazz musician must know) and know the songs in all twelve keys. He must be fluent in different styles of music. So not only do you have to know the songs in twelve keys, you have to be able to play each song with a blues feel, then perhaps a bossa nova feel or a rock and roll feel. In other words, you must have an in-depth musical knowledge of the history and the language and play it. Developing these skills is a long journey.

Metheny continues, "Once you can do that, then don't do that." Be creative and look for your own voice, your own unique sound. When playing something original, you don't think; you stop thinking of all the musical things you know from practicing and studying for all those years, and you are to "just be; just play." You just wait, listen, and respond one beat after another. It is the ultimate "living in the moment" job. So it is with the master EMDR therapist. Stop thinking and just play!

How does one become a master EMDR therapist? Learn everything you can learn about EMDR and psychology. Read all the books and take all the courses. Learn all the integration of models while using the standard protocol on patients. You are at the starting line by understanding the nuts and bolts of your area of expertise. Mastery and fluency are essential but only a place to start. Many therapists get lost in the nuts-and-bolts stuff and do not get beyond taking a course and learning another model. They do not explore their inner self or trust their inner voice because it breaks some arbitrary rule. So many potentially great therapists remain adequate because they cling to rules as their safety net. It's not a safety net; it's a cage they stay trapped in for years.

This creates an average therapist who can demonstrate technical skills, but their inner genius is missing. Being open to this inner voice makes a great therapist; without it, most of the true power of EMDR is lost. The master therapist requires other qualities beyond listening to their inner voice.

The master EMDR therapists are flexible; they follow the client and are comfortable abandoning the plan as soon as new information opens the door to a more robust path. They are patient because the inner creative self does not adhere to the therapist or client's schedule. This therapist also has a sophisticated understanding of the material that manifests during the work. They know how to listen to the client's unconscious. They understand its language. They know that absurdity is not to be ignored. Like Einstein tells us, they know logic will get you from A to B, but imagination will take you everywhere else. Logic should be part of the journey, never the destination.

When a client walks into their session complaining about a barking dog that annoyed them today, the plan is to work on a rape; the barking dog wins. If you follow the plan rather than the client, you have made a limiting mistake and lost the chance for a mythic encounter. Once the client enters the therapist's office, their unconscious becomes an ally. It will speak to the therapist if the therapist knows the language. If they hear the client's inner language, they will soon learn that most of the time, you will have to forget their previous plan and follow the client. Always follow the client because they will tell you where and what to do. The language you will learn in this book values absurdity more than logic and reason. With new respect for the absurd, a new road into the transforming power of EMDR and the unconscious mind becomes available to you.

When a thought about Chinese medicine from something read ten years ago pops into your head, and you honor it rather than dismiss it, you are in the mythic space of the inner genius. You are beginning to understand the majesty of the human psyche. You set the stage for your client's heroic journey to their true self. You are becoming one of those few therapists who have ears to hear and are listening to that inner voice.

Beyond technical abilities, the therapist must possess wisdom. Wisdom is demonstrated by their acceptance of self, understanding of self, flexibility, sense of humor, social skills, units of human achievement, problem-solving abilities, and maturity. These components are the secret sauce that provides the potential for excellence in one's work. Being a therapist may be the only profession where older people are revered. So there is an opportunity for wisdom to present itself but certainly no guarantee.

EMDR therapists, more than any other therapists, have an opportunity to create this mythic environment because EMDR is done primarily in silence. Within this silence, the unconscious speaks. The therapists must hyperfocus on the client as they listen, beat by beat of the headphones or pass after pass of the light bar. We observe each breath of the client. The master EMDR therapist is lost in every granular aspect of each moment of the process. We are blessed with an uninterrupted hour. The ultimate mono-focused hour. The goal for the therapist is to forget everything they know about EMDR theory and psychology. As the musician who can play all the songs in every key is told "now that you can do that, don't do that," so it is with the therapist. Now that you know all that EMDR stuff, forget it all and just wait, watch, and listen.

Once the ability to stop thinking is achieved and the therapists can just wait, watch and listen, a profound connection between client and therapist occurs. It is in these moments where the true power of EMDR presents itself. And like Ryan, the inner genius will be there for you. Your Kairos Moment awaits.

CREATING THE MYTHIC ENVIRONMENT OF FLOW

B.F. Skinner was doing his experiments based on punishment and reward. His counterpart, Hungarian-American psychologist Mihaly Csikszentmihalyi, who was perhaps the first positive psychologist, was having none of this limited view of humans. He knew there was more to humans than simply seeking pleasure and avoiding pain.

Mihaly Csikszentmihalyi wanted to explore why people do things without a reward. He followed a group of painters around Chicago for months to determine if he could identify their underlying psychological process—what drives them to paint even though there is little reward.

He discovered that these artists were not interested in a reward or outcome. Creative people are not interested in the outcome. So what was the driving force of the process, if not reward or the finished product?

They do it for the process of creating something they never accomplished before, whether it's a painting, a sculpture, a poem, or climbing a mountain. One climber said, "It's nice to get to the top, but really, we just wish the climbing would go on forever." The passion for this creative process drives the behavior, not money, reward, or even the outcome. It is the process of being in flow that drives them. Being consumed by the creative process where you lose track of time, you do not know your name, you are not interested in food or sex. Csikszentmihalyi called this all-consuming singular task as being in flow.[4]

It is not unusual for an actor to never watch the final cut of their movies. It's not the movie. It's the process of inhabiting the character and playing off the other characters. Pat Metheny stated he doesn't listen to his albums once the album has gone to the presses; he is already thinking about the next one. He is ready for the new creative endeavor to begin.

Ryan was in flow, and so was his client. Flow is not an EMDR term. It might be unfamiliar to you. Flow is required to access your inner genius; flow is necessary to develop mastery that opens the door to the inner self. When I teach therapists how to create flow in their work with the client, they realize just how much unnecessary interrupting they do. Once they understand the power of flow, they stop the interruptions and things *flow* much better and faster.

Although this might be an unfamiliar term, Shapiro makes the point throughout her text that therapist's interruption is to be kept to a minimum. Somehow this idea has gotten lost over the years. Clinicians seem to be more interested in trying out their latest skill rather than allowing the self-healing power of EMDR to do the work. Additionally, clinicians who use their hands and avoid the machines for EMDR stimulation never really get their client into flow. Hard to understand why a choice that limits EMDR's power is used.

What is flow exactly?

**Three ingredients for flow to occur,
thus creating Mythic Space**

1. You must be monotasking, solely focused on one task without distractions.
2. There must be a clearly defined goal that means something to you. It must be meaningful for you to get into the state of flow.
3. It has to be at the edge of your ability. It must be doable and not overwhelmingly beyond your skill. Neither can it be so easy that there is no challenge.

Flow cannot exist with interruption. These three requirements create the environment for the person to get into flow. Flow is fragile, so distractions can end or even prevent flow. Therapists work in a rare, uninterrupted environment that creates an enormous opportunity to achieve flow. Do not mistake flow for being in the zone. Flow creates the environment for finding the zone, but it does not always happen. The cliché that creativity is

90 percent perspiration and 10 percent inspiration is true. That 90 percent happens in flow without being in the zone. The zone is where genius and creativity appear.

The beauty of providing EMDR using electronics is the client can close their eyes and lose themselves in flow. EMDR creates the flow state almost immediately. There is something quite remarkable about the process of EMDR that causes the client to immediately get into the flow. So what is so mythic about flow? Let's explore the mythic connection to creativity and genius.

INNER GENIUS AND MYTH WITHIN EMDR

To describe the heroic nature of therapy and the mythic nature of what goes on there, let's define what we mean by genius myth in the context of EMDR therapy and creativity in general.

Michael Meade tells us that the phrase "genius myth" unites two essential words that tend to be both misunderstood and diminished in the modern world. Genius is not limited to a demonstration of high levels of intelligence or a display of astonishing talent. Modern man distills the word genius down to IQ and extraordinary talent. Meade disagrees. He says, "the original meanings of genius included the entirety of traits united in a begotten being and that which is just born. Genius is, therefore, the entirety of traits and talents already existing in the soul of each person born. We are born with it. (Meade, 2016, 37)

> It is something deeply ingrained, markedly original and ultimately transcendent. Although widely accepted in traditional cultures, the idea that genius is an original spirit residing in each soul causes problems in modern society based on objectivity, rationality, and scientific methods. (Meade, 2016, 5)

When you discover your purpose, you will be able to look back and say, this all makes sense. I can see that I enjoyed this as a kid, that course I took opened my eyes to this new view, or that book impacted me more than I thought. You will not know it at the time, but when you look back on those years, you will see your slender threads. You will know and realize that your talents were always there.

In terms of myth, Michael Meade again gives a working definition of myth. Myth means "emergent truth, the truth trying to emerge from just under the skin of so-called 'reality.' Genius points to something deeply ingrained, markedly original, and ultimately transcendent in our human nature" (Meade, 2016, 5). Through contact with myth, we become more imaginative and find the subtle, symbolic ground hidden in our lives: who we are at our deepest core self. We are each genius born and mythic by nature, as genius is the mythic imprint within each one of us (Meade, 2016, 37). In other words, we are each born with the talent of our own unique genius. The challenge for most of us is to find out what this uniqueness is and how to access it and use it. Meade's optimistic view is that we are all wondrous in our own way.

Once we connect with our inner genius, we become more creative, authentic, and alive. This mythic contact reveals our genuine work and our true purpose while we are on this planet.

The price of authenticity is high. We often reject it—the hero's refusal of the call. Christ himself uttered, "Let this cup pass from me." Authenticity does not create a warm and fuzzy feeling all over. A crucifixion is required. Usually, no one comes to this voluntarily. Death of the old way must occur, and all death is painful, but it is only through this psychological death that the hero's journey to the Holy Grail can occur.

There are many models of the hero's journey; some have

twelve steps, some fourteen. Our EMDR transformational path is a six-stage process that coincides with Joseph Campbell's twelve-step journey of the hero. When clients do transformational work, the process moves through the six transformational stages, and the twelve-step journey of the hero lives within these six stages.

Myths are not stories; they are truths and innately hardwired into the human psyche. What do I mean by hardwired? Have you ever read a story or watched a movie and hoped the villain would win? Do you wish Mr. Potter won and George Bailey lost in *It's a Wonderful Life?* Did you hope Vader would just kill Skywalker? Of course not. We are hardwired to root for the protagonist. The steps of the hero's story are hardwired. We are each a hero in our own heroic journey.

The journey starts by recognizing and understanding the devastating effect that old patterns have on our life. For EMDR clinicians, this wealth of damage is expressed in a simple phrase known as a negative cognition like *I don't matter* or *I'm not good enough.* This simple phrase infiltrates every area of a person's life. The *I don't matter* person's view is everyone else matters, and they do not matter. Sadly, they are entirely unaware of this reality. These phrases are the core of our work, and identifying them begins the hero's journey.

EMDR is the antidote from the power of the negative cognition, from the suffocating lack of creativity our clients find themselves in. C.S. Lewis tells us that tyrants are all so alike, and the saints are incredibly unique and different. Each saint has access to their inner creativity, while each tyrant is stuck in what they have come to know ages ago and learned nothing new. No one dares tell the tyrant they are wrong; if you question the poisonous king's power, execution will likely follow. Therefore, no creativity, innovation, or beauty can exist there.

We experience this personally when we get stuck in our old

way of thinking and resist new ideas. A collective example of the dangers of the loss of myth and creativity is Putin's Ukrainian war. He has no use for creativity or innovation. He is fighting this Ukrainian War with the 1940 strategy and getting pulverized by a younger, innovative, and creative generation led by an inspiring, clever forty-year-old comedian who has access to his inner genius. Putin is under the spell of the poisonous king. He is lost in some historical idea of greatness that no longer exists except in the madness of his isolated mind. Zelensky is like King Arthur and Putin, like Herod, who is happy to slaughter children to keep a new generation of ideas from emerging in his country.

Robert Bly describes Jung's tension of opposites that always exists. First, the tension is between the two kings, the poisonous king and the sacred king. The poisonous king, like Herod, seeks to strip all young men and women of their creativity. Teachers can attest to this with politicians banning books and telling them what they can and cannot say in a classroom. Desolation is the effect of the poisonous king, who rules by fear and cruelty. No creativity or innovation is allowed. Everyone must think like the poisonous king. Books are banned, and teachers must abide by the suffocating presence of the poisonous king or suffer the consequences. The unchanging leader knows all the answers and only wants to hear from the proverbial "yes men."

Psychology is no different. Greed, under the motto of "managed care," takes money and provides as little care as possible. Insurance companies tell doctors and therapists what to do, when to do it, and for how long you can do it, and how much you will earn. Their oppressive system causes the most skilled and talented therapists not to accept that bargain. People who are insured get poor-quality care.

The poisonous king sells guns while kids are slaughtered in school and tells the masses lies, like more guns will make us safe

—all in the service of money and power. There are thousands of examples like this one, even in our field of psychology. Beware of the power of the poisonous king who seeks power and influence while resisting creative ideas and innovation.

Ricky Greenwald, PhD, tells the story of one of his research studies in which he proved that EMDR was more effective than Cognitive Behavioral Therapy. He submitted it to some cognitive behavioral journal where he was told they would publish it, but he'd have to change the results to show Cognitive Behavioral Therapy was as good as EMDR.

My supervisor at Florida State University, David Gitlin, PhD, noticed that a psychological testing instrument published by a world-renowned psychologist looked unreliable at first glance. It was supposed to measure thoughts, but he saw that some questions were about beliefs rather than explicit cognitions. Dr. Gitlin tested the instrument and, in his dissertation, proved it was invalid and unreliable. It was removed from the market for about six months and then made available again. You can still buy it today. An invalid and unreliable instrument but still a money maker.

Shapiro experienced the rejection of her ideas by the patriarchy of the scientific research bureaucracy. She encountered the poisonous king. "What's this waving your hand in front of someone's eyes to make them feel better? Outrageous. Crazy things come out of California; we know." If Shapiro was not as strong and determined as she was, EMDR might have just been a fad for a while, like many other ideas. Her idea was a stroke of genius. Her discovery occurred by way of access to her inner genius. This EMDR thing was innovative, creative, powerful, and unusual. Her discovery is a prime example of the power of the inner genius coming to life.

The poisonous king in our field can come in many shapes and

sizes. I attended a training to explore the idea of becoming a qualified supervisor in Florida. The trainer, Katie Lemieux, LMFT, asked, "Has anyone had a bad experience with a supervisor?"

Surprisingly, almost the entire room raised their hand, including me. The supervisor, or in the EMDR community, the consultant who trains those seeking certification or other higher credentials, has a sacred role; her questions called out the lack of ethics when there is such a power differential. The relationship between the mentor and mentee is not only sacred but also archetypal, though some supervisors do not see their role as such.

I treasured most of my supervisors; most were spectacularly ethical and wise. But the poisonous king or queen encounter is almost impossible to avoid on our journey. The hero must always be on guard for the domain of the poisonous king. These people seek power and authority for their purpose. They abuse this power and often harm the trainee when their role should be that of protector who slowly doles out more responsibility as the mentee's skill allows. Lemieux's question provided shocking results in this group of training supervisors. It was shocking to hear so many toxic stories—supervisors forcing supervisees to get their clothes from the laundry or asking to lie to a spouse to cover for the supervisor, to more severe allegations of sexual misconduct.

Charles Bukowski, the American poet, warns (excerpts):

> there is enough treachery, hatred violence absurdity in
>   the average
> human being to supply any given army on any
>   given day
>
> and the best at murder are those who preach against it
> and the best at hate are those who preach love[5]

I would add:

> *The best at lying are those who preach the truth*
> *The best at betrayal are those who preach loyalty*
> *The best at abuse are those who preach against it.*

This inner work keeps the poisonous king at bay and helps you recognize when you're in the presence of someone who works from that toxic position. Even with all the work and preparation, there is always tension between the poisonous and sacred king, King Arthur, who unites and fosters the creative mythic, mysterious energy; he embraces the new power from others, including the young. He hears and is heard. He unifies and inspires. Out of the ashes emerges the sacred king in Volodymyr Zelensky, a comedian using all the modern tools of his generation to unite the world in a fight for freedom, creativity, peace, and art. Putin hears no one and sends thousands to slaughter using old worn-out strategies and tactics. He is isolated and alone. He is the poisonous king in a corrupt blind land.

The collective societal example above and the more personal example of the mentor and mentee relationship exist within you and each of your clients. Within each of us is both the poisonous and sacred king. One might think of the uncreative aspect of the old self-represented by our original negative cognition, *I don't matter,* or *I'm not good enough.* These cognitions are the domain of the poisonous king ready to strip the creative potential away from each of us. It is C.S. Lewis's land of the white witch, where it is always winter but never Christmas.

These negative cognitions take hold early in life, sometimes at birth. Ironically, these negative cognitions helped us survive as kids but eventually failed us as adults. An adult without change is under the reign of the poisonous king. You do not have to look very far to see such people. Each of us has the choice to follow the unchanging nature of our poisonous king or change and adapt to enter the world of the sacred king toward our true authentic journey.

So how does this journey begin? Ironically, the first stage of our EMDR hero's journey starts with avoidance, "refusal of the call." There is always resistance to breaking away from the kingdom we know. This is how heroic journeys begin. We avoid them.

Francine Shapiro and C.G. Jung were aware of the problem of *avoidance* and the need to break through it to engage in the journey of Shapiro's adaptive self or Jung's individuation process. Campbell's understanding of the hero's journey also begins with a refusal of the call to adventure. It is no wonder why avoidance begins the story of our hero, our clients, and our own personal process of change.

EMDR AS THE SAFE AND SECURE VESSEL FOR THE JOURNEY

EMDR is an evidence-based therapy. There have been over five hundred EMDR studies. Over forty of them are randomized, controlled longitudinal studies. EMDR has a solid structure in its eight-phase model. This vessel of EMDR creates the safe process for the transformational work of our clients. Although not always known by the uninitiated, EMDR has about seven or eight ways to design the process that expands or limits the amount of material a client processes on any given day. This factor strengthens the safety aspect of the journey. EMDR, unlike many other therapies, has an off-ramp for the client. We have Phase Two: Resourcing, which allows the client to stop at any time within the session and calm themselves with strategies we put in place.

We can consider our vessel of EMDR as Hans Solo's *Millennium Falcon,* the fastest ship in the galaxy. Additionally, the client has a map. The six stages of transformation allow the client to know where they are, where they are going and where they have been. Seeing through the lens of the twelve steps of the hero further motivates and reassures the client. Finally, because the therapist knows the map, the client is assured that the therapist has been on this journey before and knows the way.

Once this is all in place, the space for the mythic hero's journey can begin.

CHAPTER 3
TRANSFORMATIONAL STAGE ONE: AVOIDANCE
THE HERO'S FIRST STEPS ON THE JOURNEY

E very myth has a story with several characters. In EMDR therapy, the client is the hero. This is not a metaphor for EMDR therapy. The hero is an archetype, and an archetype is innate.

Whereas metaphors are the building blocks of language, archetypes form part of the common groundwork of human emotion. Archetypes, composed of universal stories and images, have been recognized in Western culture since Aristotle analyzed Sophocles' tragic hero in Oedipus Rex. Their provenance is not an accident of cultural evolution. They are part of deep history, obedient to instinctive genetic biases acquired through evolution by natural selection. Some of their ultimate causes date back tens of thousands of years to a time when humans were spreading out from Africa to all the habitable globe.[1]

THE TWELVE STEPS of the hero's journey exist within the six stages of transformation that EMDR ignites. This process is also innate. As E.O. Wilson suggests, the six stages that EMDR clients move through are indeed innate and genetically based. They are hardwired into the human experience. The steps and stages define the archetypal journey we all must take to fulfill our lives. Even if we refuse the call, this refusal is an archetypal option and is still true to one's personal mythology.

These scenes are instinctual when the hero encounters a cliff's edge and confronts death or when Indiana Jones is in a pit full of snakes. Humans fear heights and snakes. Filmmakers are acutely aware of this reality. We know to stay safe, we should avoid snakes and heights.

These evolutionary fears are not part of the archetypal journey by chance. They are a force of nature. Myths are archetypal stories that represent our individual life's journey. EMDR is an incredible vessel for that journey.

It is no wonder the *Star Wars* movies resonated with such power from one generation to another. Lucas used Joseph Campbell's descriptions of the Hero's Journey as a map for his *Star Wars* script. EMDR takes the client on their archetypal journey as the therapist accompanies the clients through the steps and stages of their heroic life's journey.

Francine Shapiro and C.G. Jung discuss the six stages of transformation, although they never really explained them as a six-stage process. This process was my EMDR discovery. We will look at their perspective later. In my previous book, the six-stage parallel was compared to the death and resurrection of Christ. Christ, too, traveled this six-stage model.

In this book, we will explore the six stages of transformation through the eyes of the hero's journey, as described by Joseph Campbell. Within this mythic view, we will see the value of

Jungian psychology and EMDR therapy. When these models are combined, the client accelerates and understands the arduous path of transformation under the care of the EMDR therapist, who has this mythological experience of Jung and the scientific knowledge of Shapiro to ensure the client completes their journey.

Six Stages of Transformation with Christian Parallel

1. Avoidance: Let this cup pass from me.
2. Surrender: Not my will but yours
3. Dismantling the old self: Crucifixion
4. Loss of identity: Chaos and confusion—panic sets in after His death
5. Rebirth: Resurrection
6. Acceptance of the new self: Ascension[2]

Joseph Campbell examines a number of steps and stages of the hero in literature. He shares his conclusions in his book *The Hero with A Thousand Faces*.

For our purposes, we are using a twelve-step model common to most heroic myths. These twelve steps exist in my six stages of transformation. This chapter explores the twelve steps of the hero's journey within the six-stage transformational EMDR process.

Campbell's Twelve-Step Journey of the Hero

1. The Ordinary World
2. The Call to Adventure
3. The Refusal of the Call
4. Meeting the Mentor

   5. Crossing the Threshold
   6. Tests, Allies, and Enemies
   7. Approach of the Innermost Cave
   8. The Supreme Ordeal
   9. Reward, Seizing the Sword
  10. The Road Back
  11. Resurrection
  12. Return with the Elixir

THE HERO'S STEP ONE: THE ORDINARY WORLD

Transformational EMDR Stage One: Avoidance

CAMPBELL'S first step of the hero's journey is called *the ordinary world*. This descriptor refers to the world of the client's daily life. This is Luke Skywalker harvesting his uncle's crops, living a peaceful, ordinary yet unfulfilling life.

In the life of an *I don't matter* hero, the crops matter, the harvest matters, and his uncle and aunt matter, but he does not, even though the *I matter* part of Luke is crying out to be released. He is stuck in the ordinary world and submits to this mundane reality. Once the client is with the therapist in session, the client has an opportunity to leave *the ordinary world* to potentially enter the mythic world and begin the hero's journey. They have been invited to leave the old way by allowing the EMDR therapist to help them dismantle the old self that is no longer working for them, to cut ties with the poisonous king. The invitation is usually a problem that the client cannot figure out, so they seek assistance.

A highly skilled EMDR therapist knows the problem is far beyond the overt symptoms. I hope this book will encourage

EMDR therapists to stop looking for the next new protocol that someone made up in their basement and start looking within the self-healing power of EMDR by better understanding what's going on right in front of your eyes.

It is essential to understand that the work done in the therapist's office is a microcosm of what will happen in the macrocosm of the client's life. After a few sessions, EMDR creates the energy that will cause cataclysmic change within the client's world, the macrocosm. These steps and stages have one meaning in the therapist's office and another in the client's world. The prison of the poisonous king's ordinary life will die as the extraordinary journey is waiting to be born, like Frodo enjoying his ordinary world in the shire when word comes that a war is brewing and evil forces are at work, or Obi-Wan's declaration there is trouble in the force. This is when the hero's ordinary life is disrupted. The skilled EMDR therapist understands that the client who cannot understand why they feel so much distress is meeting their unconscious in adversarial mode. The unconscious will not be denied. You can only avoid your reality for so long, and then the adversary attacks.

The hero's *ordinary world* occurs within our transformation stage one—Avoidance. No matter the symptoms or diagnosis, the problem is that the client's old way of doing things is no longer working. It has worked for decades, but now change is required. The methods of behavior that the client has been using since they were a child and young adult do not work as an adult. Change is needed, but the client has no idea what that means or what kind of change is required.

The Transformational EMDR™ therapist understands the situation perfectly because they understand that a negative cognition is born in childhood for each and every one of us. It sets the stage for the quest, this hero's journey. This disruption is uncomfortable for the client. Otherwise, the client would not seek help.

The skilled EMDR therapist understands the difference between negative cognition and transformational negative cognition. They keenly understand these two categories of cognitions must be handled differently. The skilled EMDR therapist knows the power of transformational negative cognition and understands the inherent dangers of employing such a cognition. You must never employ this cognition without consulting and explaining the implication to your client. These cognitions are a call to adventure, and the hero must accept the call. It is your job to explain the implications of this heroic journey so the client can make an informed decision. These cognitions can create immediate and permanent change, while less robust negative cognitions limit the amount of material processed in a session with a less dramatic effect. Understanding the differences in power between these two categories of negative cognitions is essential for effective EMDR processing. The skilled therapist has an acute understanding of ordinary time and the danger of awakening the poisonous king, but awaken he must.

The transformational cognition is like dynamite. It has the potential to blow up the client's entire world. This destruction is in the service of creating the authentic path. It can still be cataclysmic. The life of "ignorance is bliss" disappears. The client realizes that living a life driven by their negative cognition means, for example, they've been doing everything everyone wanted them to do while never asking, "What do I want?" They now know they live in the realm of the poisonous king. Here the client receives the call to the adventure. Death of the old way must happen for the new way to begin. This book is about the destruction of the old way, the old self, allowing rebirth to occur. This dismantling is required so the new authentic life journey begins. When EMDR is employed, death can happen suddenly and unexpectedly.

IDENTIFYING THE NEGATIVE COGNITION AND THE LAND OF THE POISONOUS KING

There are only two transformational cognitions. Dr. Sue Johnson, the developer of *Emotionally Focused Couples Therapy*, states that 85 percent of couples that come in for couples therapy have one person who has the negative cognition, *I'm not good enough.* The other partner's cognition is, *I don't matter.* The remaining 15 percent of the couples have two *I don't matter* people or two *I'm not good enough* people in the relationship.[3]

When I heard Dr. Johnson share this information, I was shocked. It changed everything. My understanding of the negative cognitions changed. My perception of my clients changed. This new understanding unleashed a new power of EMDR that was previously hidden from me and everyone else. This new transformational capability of EMDR for my clients was enormous. EMDR previously had the power of a flashlight, and now it has the power of a lightning bolt. It can now ignite the transformational journey of the hero in my little office in Sebastian, Florida, where I provide a transformational environment for my clients where they can engage their hero's journey, seeking their true authentic selves.

The reason these cognitions are so powerful is these transformational cognitions contain many other cognitions within. For example, when EMDR is administered, the client is asked to free-associate. A sample instruction is:

"Let whatever wants to happen, happen."

"Do not try to make anything happen, and do not prevent anything from happening."

"Just free-associate."

We begin with a troubling image and the appropriate negative cognition. For example, let's say your mother was disappointed in your performance on a report card. Her comment, "If you would study like your brother, you wouldn't have gotten that *C*." The negative cognition paired with this event is *I'm not good enough*. As the process starts, the client's mind will move at the speed of thought through the client's life. This can include other narrower cognitions like, *I'm stupid, I should have known better, I'm a geek, I'm just dumb, the teacher hates me, I'm too fat, I'm too slow*, etc. Any thoughts, feelings, images, memories, or body sensations related to an experience of *I'm not good enough* can come to mind during processing. Activating transformational cognitions can be overwhelming for the client. It is a heavy lift to accept that they have lived the last forty years treating themselves and allowing others to treat them like they are not good enough.

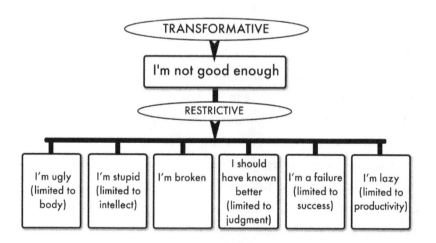

You can see that the more restrictive negative cognitions within the transformation cognition are in the bottom row. Using one of the NCs in the bottom row limits how much material gets processed.

In the graphics are examples of the transformational cognition and the more restrictive cognitions.

Sometimes the therapist may choose to limit processing so the session is not overwhelming by not using the all-encompassing *I'm not good enough* cognition. We paired the mother's statement with a less robust cognition like *I'm stupid*. Usually, the processing associations with this cognition will be about the mom or school. These choices are not a guarantee, but using *I'm stupid* does reduce the amount of material to process, rather than *I'm not good enough*. The narrower cognitions live within *I'm not good enough*. This strategy gives the clinician control over how much material is processed without interfering in the process.

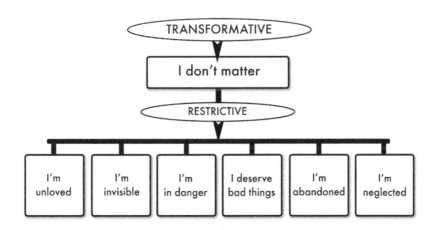

How are these transformational cognitions created? These are powerful because they develop at an early age. Humans are designed for this to happen. If a kindergarten teacher yells at the five-year-old in front of the class, there is a devastating and immediate response in the child's nervous system. The child feels embarrassed. The child doesn't think:

"She must have argued with her husband."

"This isn't about me; it's her."

Children do not have the cognitive ability to defend themselves in that way. The child internalizes this moment and thinks, *I'm stupid. Everyone else is better than me. I am different. I'm alone. No one else made that mistake. What's wrong with me?* Then our human biology kicks in, designed to protect us so this never happens again. Our sympathetic nervous system immediately goes into action, firing a flush of neurotransmitters activating the brain's emotional center, creating shame, shock, fear, and embarrassment along with the more primitive part of the brain where the fight-flight-freeze response goes into action, and bam! The core belief is up and running. Within the magnificence of this biological machinery, the child gets the message: DON'T FORGET THIS! The child never does forget it. Their life's purpose is to make sure that it never happens again. They take extraordinary efforts to make sure getting shamed and embarrassed like that never happens again.

Behaviors immediately change, and then *I'm not good enough* self-perception is born along with all its problems. What are the new behaviors that keep them safe? What ensures this never happens again? The child is under the rule of the poisonous king. They make sure they do everything like everyone else. They never question authority. They make sure their paper looks just like everyone else's—no chance of creativity or innovation. Fear and cruelty extinguished that possibility. No coloring out of the lines for this kid ever again. These behaviors continue because they work. These "do what everyone else does to avoid trouble" behaviors have kept the child safe from shame.

Although being invisible and passive is effective in school as a child, these once-effective behaviors now as an adult are ineffective. Others will take advantage of you, and you will let them. You will take less challenging and exciting positions for fear of failing and being shamed again. The behaviors that once served you as a child are now detrimental. In adulthood, the transformational negative cognition of *I'm not good enough* becomes overwhelming and creates havoc in every area of the client's life. The client continues this behavior because they do not know any other way. For the most part, the negative core belief kept them safely away from shame. The problem is no one tells the child, now an adult, that they must change. The client will live under the domain of the poisonous king of *not being good enough* for the rest of their life unless they receive *the call*.

My wife and I are in Sue Johnson's 15 percent group of couples. We are both *I'm not good enough* people. I was the first male born in our family, so I was treated like I mattered, and my wife was the first girl born after four boys. She knew she mattered, but neither of us felt like we were ever good enough. My negative belief began in my mother's womb. My mom's family were immigrants; like most immigrants, they came to America for a better life. They settled in a small steel town, were very poor, and were discriminated against. My mother was also the middle child. Her older brother was favored by her mother. My journey was set in stone before I was born.

To further exacerbate my entry into the world, I was born prematurely. On the day I was born, *I was weak; I was a disappointment. I was different*, and certainly, *I was not good enough*. I was separated from all the healthy kids crying in the nursery and placed alone in an incubator. The die was cast before my parents ever met me. Feeling like I was good enough was going to be my life's work. My quest was in place.

So it is with you and everyone else walking around the world.

We come in with a negative belief about ourselves and must work through it to see clearly past this maladaptive view to find the authentic self that will show us our true purpose.

I explore in my first book the insidious nature of the negative core belief. Briefly, the reason it is insidious is that the negative cognitions are often born out of strength, wits, and awareness. Let's say an abusive alcoholic is raising a child. Children of alcoholic parents carry the negative cognition, *I don't matter*. Alcohol mattered, and the child did not matter. The child knows keeping quiet and not making waves is a way to stay safe. The child learns early on that it is wise to be invisible and, if possible, to disappear metaphorically and physically at the sign of any high emotion by going to a friend's house to avoid chaos. These behaviors are adaptive and keep the child safe. The problem is this manner of coping does not work for adults.

As an adult, the strategy of running away any time there is high emotion no longer works, but the client knows no other way. They cannot be passive when someone takes advantage of them to avoid distressing emotions, but they are. If one is passive as an adult, you will be taken advantage of in all areas of your life. Your spouse will take advantage of you, and friends, family, and colleagues will take advantage of you. The motto the *I don't matter* person lives by is everyone else matters, and I do not matter.

HERO'S JOURNEY STEP TWO: THE CALL TO ADVENTURE

The first stage is avoidance, which can last for decades, perpetuating a toxic *ordinary world* reality. We use denial, intellectualization, or distraction to keep the problem at bay. The insidious nature of this reality is we are completely unaware this is happening to us. We see the world as we have always understood it. We live our lives as we always lived until something happens to shake our ordinary world up. Being taken advantage of and chronically not mattering to everyone has its limit. Being passed over for promotions and needs being ignored by family take their toll. You will take less challenging and exciting positions for fear of failing and being shamed again. There can be more acute problems like experiencing depression and despair or more severe problems like panic attacks or irrational phobias, to name a few.

The client is immediately told the good news. They are told that they have gotten an invitation to transform their lives. They are invited to discover their authentic self and true purpose, and in this trade-off of dismantling the old way to make way for the new way. The six-stage process is explained to them, and a map of the journey is described in detail. Often, they don't believe that EMDR will perform as promised, nor do they understand entirely. Still, their unconscious has created such emotional distress that they are usually willing to try anything to feel better. They are the reluctant hero who eventually heeds the call. Sometimes they find this information too good to be true, but a sparkle of hope often appears in their eyes.

What happens when you employ transformational cognition using EMDR therapy? Perhaps the most visible example of what happens when you use one of the transformation cognitions with a client is Prince Harry. Prince Harry stated that EMDR therapy saved his life. I am not privy to his specific work with his therapist, but EMDR is like a flowing river. It finds its way to the true destination. Our psyche longs to be healed; once EMDR begins, there is no stopping it. The unconscious will not be denied. Harry, perhaps more than almost anyone on the planet, is an *I don't matter* person.

He is the "spare to the heir." He has been told where to go and what to do his entire life. He does not matter. The queen matters. The king matters. The monarch matters. The kingdom matters.

England matters. His duties matter. His brother matters. Harry, not so much. Harry was brave enough to take on the hero's journey; as you may have noticed, it comes at a cost. He gave up his family, title, country, and kingdom. Amazing that some call him spoiled and selfish. He is presently in stage four—loss of identity. It takes time to figure out his true purpose. He is the hero in the royal family's story, but no one will see it. All the more reason for seeking his true purpose rather than everyone telling him what it is.

HERO'S STEP THREE: REFUSING, THEN ACCEPTING THE CALL

Joseph Campbell states that the next step is the *call to adventure*. The refusal of the call almost immediately follows this call. He explains that the hero first rejects the call before deciding to take the journey. However, this temporary rejection of the call is not the same as refusing the call completely. We know there is a high price to pay for accepting the call, but the cost of refusing the call is a permanent tragedy.[4]

Sometimes the call is imposed upon the hero and there is no choice but to respond and take up the cause. What do I mean? As I was finishing this book, my younger son, John, died in an accident. He was thirty-one, extremely successful, a millionaire at thirty with people twice his age under him. He was a genius at his job. Nothing good comes from a telephone call at 4 a.m., and I was thrust into the midst of this mythic storm. A heroic journey was underway. A journey I had no choice in choosing or refusing. This horror was forced upon me, my wife, and my older son.

I told my son many times, "John, you need to slow down, or you'll die before you're forty." If you have not noticed, kids do not listen to their parents. Here I am, like Daedalus making wings for my son, warning him not to get too close to the sun because the wax holding the feathers will melt, and so it is. My son lived his brief life too close to the sun. Again, mythology warns us of these realities, realities we are all helpless to stop sometimes, but the journey must continue.

I had to answer this horrific call, which I have done and will probably continue to struggle through for quite some time. Luke Skywalker had no choice but to answer the call after his aunt and uncle were killed by stormtroopers, leaving him alone in the world. The pattern of the heroic journey resonates with us all because we all live this journey in our lives. No one gets out of here without suffering. When suffering is seen within the myth, it is endurable. The mythic nature of our lives gives suffering meaning and gives us all strength to endure almost anything.

In his book *Iron John,* Robert Bly explains the reality of "Ashes and Grief," what he calls katabasis, what we know as failure that brings desolation, despair, and defeat. Once the restaurant owner fails, losing everything, and is now washing the dishes in someone else's restaurant, only then can the soul enter. He says, "The soul enters through a wound delivered in the right place, at the right time, and in the right company."[5]

There is no way out of this wound. The client cannot buy themselves out of it. It is a "damned if you do, damned if you don't" situation. All choices are wrong. These lose-lose positions are when clients come to see therapists. In the Fisher King myth, the king is wounded. As a young man, he went out into the wilderness and met some people by a campfire. They were cooking salmon over the fire. The king took a bite and burned his fingers and his mouth. His wounds are so severe he cannot live, but he is not capable of dying. This story often relates to a client who has been betrayed or experienced an injustice. This event created the Fisher King wound.[6] The kingdom is desolate and, in this desolation and desperation, the invitation to change comes.

If we look at our clients from this perspective, they have been invited to this quest because they experienced a wound, a sacred transformation wound. This Fisher King wound can be like the devoted wife whose husband unexpectedly says he wants a divorce after twenty-five years of marriage, or the devoted young Christian student who goes off to medical school only to find she is pregnant with an unwanted pregnancy. It can be a businessperson whose partner left with all the money. It can be something less defined, like someone who walks in and says something is wrong, but I don't know what or why I do not feel like myself. I do not have a problem in the world, but I am miserable.

There are many faces to the hero's call, but one thing they all have in common. The call is born from a wound. A wound deep and bloody is not only delivered at the right time, in the right place, but also delivered by the right person. A severe wound, like the wound of the Fisher King, is a wound so profound that you cannot live, but you cannot die either—a fate worse than death. When someone says they want to change and feel warm and fuzzy, it is a good time to remember the cost of authenticity and change is high.

Therapists read books by other therapists. We therapists all know the same nothing or the same something. There is no doorway to mythic space in those therapy books. Many great writers and poets see the cost of this journey and describe it masterfully. Let's see what they have to say about the wound. In their work, they describe the treacherous nature of the journey and the magnificence of completing it.

There is a lack of poetic motivation in our work. It's all scientific. Perhaps it is missing in the world too. William Carlos Williams was right when he said,

It is difficult
to get the news from poems
yet men die miserably every day
for lack
of what is found there.

Charles Bukowski also understood the journey and the price of authenticity, the price the true path costs. He says:

this could mean losing girlfriends,
wives, relatives, jobs and
maybe your mind.

go all the way.
it could mean not eating for 3 or
4 days.
it could mean freezing on a
park bench.
it could mean jail, alcoholism,
it could mean derision,
mockery,
isolation.

He continues, about the completion of the journey:

if you're going to try,
go all the way.
there is no other feeling like it.
you will be alone with the gods
and the nights will flame with
fire. ...

you will ride death straight to
hell,
your perfect laughter,
the only good fight
now. [7]

In his book *Healing and Wholeness*, Jungian analyst John Sanford provides examples of the price for the journey to the true self. He warns, "Anything rejected by the unconscious turns against us; on the other hand, to give conscious energy to the contents of the unconscious is to begin to win their positive energy and support from within" (Sanford, 2016, 94).

He continues describing the cost of the journey. "To accept the unconscious as a partner in life is like letting in both God and the devil. It is the unconscious that carries the divine, but it also carries with it our dark, inferior part of ourselves. All that we fear and deny about ourselves is there as well" (Sanford, 1977, 100).

Jung said the unconscious is amoral. It is not moral. What does that mean? It means it does not create the news; it reports it in dreams using its own language. It is incapable of deceit. My son died on August 1, 2022, while I was writing this book. Two nights after his death, I had the following dream.

Dream No. 1, August 3, 2022

I was going to a friend's house. The front porch was a little cluttered. I was ready to knock on their door. I was stepping carefully because of the clutter there. I noticed I did not have any shoes. I was barefoot. I heard and saw our friend Laura working in the kitchen, and Randy was in his office. I told her I needed one thing from Randy, and the dream ended before I spoke to him.

Sanford tells us that being barefoot in a dream is a rare striking dream motif that may symbolize the possibility of acquiring a firm and natural psychological and spiritual standpoint that is uniquely their own. He continues there is an ancient tradition that the spirit enters and leaves us not through the head but through the feet, for which reason we still speak of the "soles" (souls) of our feet. Another old belief is that the feet are connected to the power to heal. A child who was born feet first was thought to have special healing powers.[8]

Robert Bly tells us in *A Little Book on the Shadow* that ancient wisdom says if you love and worship God, you might come to an understanding of him in about twenty or thirty years. Still, if you hate God, you can do that same work in two years.[9] Well, I put in my time on the thirty- to forty-year work trying to understand God, to understand life and my true purpose. Now, as I write these words, I'm about a month into the two-year term of hating God. We'll see how that goes.

Perhaps the unconscious gave me such a wonderful dream in my bare feet. After about forty-five years of trying, I get that dream that informs me that I possess my own unique and firm psychological and spiritual standpoint in my worldview. It is not much of a consolation. Jung's union of opposites holds true. My soul sends me a wonderful dream of inner accomplishment, so to speak, two days after my beloved son's tragic and unexpected death.

This dream gave me some hope I would get through it and help my wife and son get through such an unbearable loss. The dream reminded me that I had the strength to get through it, even though I did not believe it. The nightmares soon followed—a reflection of my reality. So you get the whole "the unconscious is amoral" is no joke. The unconscious does not play games. When Sanford says, "To engage the unconscious is like letting in God and the devil simultaneously" (Sanford, 1977, 100), he is not joking.

Experiencing that dream at the time of my son's death is a prime example of this tension between the opposites. To be on a heroic journey yet again, yes, I am forced to carry on, and it is taking a Herculean effort; it is the most important and difficult journey of my life to carry on after the worst personal tragedy of my life. Fortunately, I have my Obi-Wan to get me through it, who is my own EMDR therapist. I also love my wife, son, and friends, which helps me look ahead. It is no wonder clients try to avoid this process. It sucks, but it is the only good fight there is.

In *The Hero with a Thousand Faces*, Joseph Campbell states, "Often in actual life, and not infrequently in myths and popular tales, we encounter the dull cases of the call unanswered, for it is always possible to turn the ear to other interests" (Campbell, 1949, 59). Now more than ever, our society provides options to entertain ourselves to death. The unanswered call is an epidemic. This call is a journey toward authenticity, which only comes through self-awareness, self-examination, and the motivation to change, followed by the required changes. Answering the call is not falling into some conspiracy theory. Answering the call is spotting a conspiracy theory when something fraudulent is presented to you.

The Gnostics warn of the danger of refusing the call. "If you bring forth what is within you, what you bring forth will save you. If you do not bring forth what is within you, it will destroy you" (Meade, 2016, 36). EMDR as a process does precisely that. It brings forth that which is hidden within. From the internal depth, the old negative cognition dies psychologically, so the new adaptive cognition can come from within and save the client.

The EMDR therapist must deliver the call with sophistication and understanding to head off yet another bout of avoidance. This is done by first providing an explanation of what EMDR is and how powerfully it performs. The therapist describes the transformational negative cognitions, where they began, how and why they perpetuate their problems, and how EMDR will correct these behaviors that no longer work for the client. Whether the client accepts or refuses the call often depends on the skill of the EMDR therapist in educating the client about this process of transformation.

If there is a refusal of the call after a visit to a therapist, the unconscious seems less patient and will not let the avoidance continue. Its adversarial approach will become more aggressive. Often their symptoms worsen to the point of total despair, where they return to therapy with a "Please help me, I'll do anything" attitude.

I told my story in my first book but will briefly recount it here to demonstrate my avoidance, followed by an attack from the unconscious to ensure I would take up my call. As I was an undergraduate studying music in Chicago, my best friend John was studying literature at Notre Dame, about eighty miles from Chicago; he took a class on dream interpretation taught by Morton T. Kelsey, an Episcopal minister, Jungian analyst, and author. He was very excited about the material and suggested I start recording my dreams so we could talk about them.

As I said earlier, I was not a gifted musician, and music school was challenging for me. I did not need my dreams telling me what a mess I was at night. I already knew that in the light of day. John accepted my refusal.

That night I had the most terrifying dream of my life. The next night I had the same nightmare again until I was afraid to go to sleep with the lights off by the third night. The nightmare continued. I think this nightmare is what they call a lucid dream these days. In this dream, I am in the actual apartment I was living in at the time. I am in my bed, and I can see the time on my clock in the dream, which is the actual alarm clock and the actual time in the middle of the night. The only thing that was not real was that Lee Harvey Oswald was jumping on my bed, laughing at me, and creating a hurricane of wind and destruction in the nightmare.

I was about eight when Kennedy died, and Oswald was the most terrifying person to me as a kid and into my teens and early twenties. He was an image of archetypal evil for me, and there he was, jumping up and down on my bed in my little Chicago apartment.

Since John was the only person who knew anything about dreams, I asked him if he had any advice. He said he would ask Morton, his professor. Morton suggested I write the nightmare down in a notebook and start recording my dreams like John had asked me a week earlier. I thought this was the stupidest thing I had ever heard. "How is that going to do anything?" I didn't do it. I *avoided* his advice, and the nightmare continued until I gave up, thinking, "What have I got to lose?"

Once I recorded the nightmare, it stopped. I was afraid that it might return, so I continued to record my dreams and discuss them with John. I did this for the next twenty years with John. If you read my first book, you know just how important John was to me, especially in terms of the inner work of which we were both passionate students in our life.

My refusal of the call to work with my dreams is an example of my initial avoidance. Immediately, the unconscious's adversarial behavior started with the nightmare.

John and I discussed dream work intensely for years together. Without the dream work, our relationship would not have been half of what it was—one of my earliest slender threads. It demonstrates how the psyche responds to avoidance. Sometimes it lets you get away with it, and sometimes it comes roaring at you.

Once the invitation is delivered, it is time to meet the hero's companion.

I was so fortunate to have John as a companion throughout my life. Not many people are interested in self-discovery. If you do it properly, you will learn many things about yourself you would rather not know. John and I journaled together through adulthood and shared our dreams, life, and families until life became busy. We always kept in touch as we made our places in the world.

As I write this, John has passed away. I spoke to him before he passed, and he told me he was at peace and unafraid. He said, "Thanks for being my soul friend. No one gets many, and some get none. I am grateful we grew up a block away from one another." John died on July 31, 2022, and less than twenty-four hours after that, my younger son John died unexpectedly. There has never been a time in my life when I longed to talk to my deceased friend for his counsel and comfort about the horrific loss of my son. When I needed his support, he was not there for the first time in my life. Both he and my son died on nearly the same day.

Sometimes you do not get to refuse the call. Sometimes it is thrust upon you, and you must decide to fight, hang on, or give up and die. I chose the former.

HERO STEP FOUR: MEETING THE COMPANION—THE EMDR THERAPIST

In the hero's journey, there is always a companion to help with the challenges. When we think of *The Lord of the Rings,* we know Frodo had Sam, Frodo's ever-present companion, looking after the hero. Luke Skywalker immediately runs into Obi-Wan, the wise sage, his companion who will teach him the ways of the Force.

There is a myth about Pythias and his dedicated friend Damon in Greek mythology. In this story, Pythias is accused of plotting against the tyrannical Dionysius of Syracuse. Pythias requests that Dionysius allow him to settle his affairs before his execution. Dionysius agrees on one condition: He insists Pythias's friend Damon be held hostage and, should Pythias not return, Damon will be executed in his stead. When Pythias returns, Dionysius, amazed by the love and trust in their friendship, frees them both.

You are your client's Obi-Wan or Frodo's Sam. You are Pythias's dedicated companion Damon. You have accompanied many who took this road, bringing them to the new life. You are the one who knows what to expect, how to stay safe and not get lost on the journey.

In my first book, I made the point that as an EMDR therapist, I stopped feeling like a psychologist and more like a midwife, giving new life to clients on their mythic journey. During EMDR therapy, the journey is abbreviated but no less arduous. With EMDR, the primary challenge is to let go of an old way of thinking and behaving and move to an adaptive and healthy way of behaving and thinking. It is not so much as a midwife but as the hero's companion along the journey. The relationship is archetypal, but it is usually seen as a person administering treatment for a diagnosis and sending the client on their way as soon and as cheaply as possible. Once psychotherapy was under the reign of the medical model, its soul was lost. Here we are trying to rekindle the magic within each of us.

THE SKILLS OF THE MENTOR

Heroes not only have a companion, but there is also an overarching sage who oversees and guides the process.

As we build our story with our cast of characters, we notice a three-tier relationship. We have the patient, the therapist, and the supervisor or consultant. To be clear, the patient is the hero (i.e., Luke Skywalker or Frodo). The therapist is Obi-Wan or Frodo's Sam or Pythias's Damon, the companion who keeps the hero safe. The consultant or supervisor to the therapist would be Gandalf or Yoda, the sage-like teacher who holds all the wisdom needed to assist with the journey. Of course, people can joke and laugh about these comparisons. If you stop seeing yourself as the all-knowing therapist with a plan and more of a companion waiting for the hero to tell you where the adventure will take him, your effectiveness and transforming power as a therapist will increase dramatically.

Let's examine the relationship between the therapist and the supervisor and set the patient aside for the moment. These two often find themselves at opposite ends of the circle of life or at least opposite ends of their therapeutic experience. One is close to the end of their career and sometimes even their life, and the other is closer to the beginning of their career. If this relationship develops appropriately, the mentee can become wiser than their age might suggest, and the mentor can experience a youthful renewal that the mentee provides. Within the sacred respect of this relationship, both can activate their creative inner genius. Both can enter the relationship not knowing some hidden things, and as the relationship progresses, both will learn something about themselves and each other that neither knew before the relationship. This relationship does not happen in the domain of the poisonous king.

The mentor, if genuine, appears as the opposite of those who have power but use it unjustly, as we observed with some toxic supervisors. This toxic mentor has positional authority; they have the power to make or break you, and they will use that power.

The genuine mentor has inner authority and draws upon a

deeper sense of authenticity. The genuine mentor uses their power to benefit others. One serves themselves and the demands of the moment, and the other serves others, the unforeseen future, and aims to awaken the mentee's soul to learn to do the same when their time comes (Meade, 2018, 133).

In his book *The Genius Myth,* Michael Meade tells us, "Mentoring involves a mythic sense that individual life repeatedly transforms and the understanding that with each generation the world must be made anew. Mentoring is a renewable practice with roots in the human soul, a prototypical way of learning and teaching that can bring genuinely inspired ideas and heartfelt dreams that can alter the conditions of the world."

If you haven't noticed, the world can use some alterations. We ask, "What can I do to change the world?" I can mentor with a mythic responsibility that activates genuinely inspired ideas and heartfelt dreams in others; one by one, we alter the world's condition.

Encouraging the mythic sensibility in this mentorship journey adds an artistic and mysterious quality to the process. This does not mean science is neglected. Nothing is taken away, but the relationship's richness is added. So often, psychology is seen solely through the scientific lens. Knowing the rubrics of the EMDR process, understanding trauma, learning to manage dissociation, adding a little parts work and ego state therapy cover the curriculum for the mentee, the consultant in training (CIT). These efforts only get you to a place to start. Now that you can do all that, don't do that, as we discussed earlier. Education has three stages, and learning the language of the discipline is a necessary part of becoming a master at your skill. Remember, the goal is to forget everything you know and just wait, watch, and listen. Only when you learn to stop thinking can you be completely present, opening the door for the inner genius to manifest when you need that brilliant inner part of ourselves that we all posses. So know that you know all of that stuff; when you are in front of your client, forget it and just wait, watch and listen.

True mentoring encourages the consultee to take their own hero's journey. True mentorship invites a deep exploration into the inner realm of the consultee's self. Journaling, dream work, and the trainee's EMDR work should be required. True mentorship explores the latest research and the mystery uncovered by men like Jung, Freud, and other early pioneers.

It is best to seek a mentor who you suspect knows secret things. It is hard to determine who knows secret things, but it is probably not the person out in front of everyone running around all over the place doing all sorts of different things. Genuine mentors are not looking for attention or people to tell them how great they are. They are also very discerning. They do not let just anyone into their world. They are aware of the secrets they possess. They know it took a lifetime to learn, and most of the lessons have nothing to do with EMDR, and that's the greatest secret.

To be a master EMDR therapist is about 10 percent EMDR skills and 90 percent understanding everything else. The same thing that makes a great therapist makes a great mentor: a sense of humor, and if it is self-deprecating, so much the better. They must be flexible and mature. The mentor should be interested in learning from you as much as you are interested in learning from them. There should be a real sense that there is something precious behind the curtain, something you know you cannot get anywhere else. The mentor's purpose, as previously stated, is not to wield power but to create a safe environment for the trainee to be relaxed enough to do their best work. The mentor brings out the best in the trainee, creating access to their inner genius—that creative self within.

"The grandness of life must be represented to young people through someone other than their parents" (Meade, 2016, 133). I can only be my son's father. I cannot be his priest, therapist, mentor, or friend. I cannot be his savior. I'm just his dad. Nor can I be my client's friend or savior. I am their therapist—one hour at a time for which I am paid. Mentorship is desperately needed in our world, and a parent cannot do that work for their children. In our world of "I have to be number one," the environment is ripe for betrayal and abuse. The mentee is often naïve and is ripe for being betrayed. One must carefully tread when choosing a mentor. Talk to others who have gone before you.

A final message for the aging expert who takes on the role of mentoring the young apprentice:

- Talent is to be given to others.
- Your life experience is to be shared with others.
- Your secrets are to be shared with others.

This sharing does not mean your talent and wisdom are given to everyone and certainly not to just anyone who asks, for it is written, "Do not throw pearls before swine." The mentor's discernment decides with whom the secrets are shared.

One of the essential roles of a mentor is to prepare their replacements. This sharing is difficult for some. Perhaps a visible example is when an aging quarterback is asked to mentor the young quarterback. Different men in this position respond differently. Some embrace the role, and others have nothing but disdain for that role. Some hang on too long, and some are self-aware enough to know when to let go.

For mental health professionals, it should be a little easier. For the therapist, mentoring becomes a new job. We are not put out to pasture. In fact, psychotherapy may be one of the few jobs where age is revered and respected. The resistance to sharing their secrets and genuinely teaching the mentee comes from older mentors who are insecure, who fear that the new therapist will take their client away or know more than the mentor. This is all driven by the cognition *I'm not good enough.* If the mentor has done their inner work and worked with their own EMDR therapist, this does not happen. Keep this in mind: If you are on the fence about taking this in-depth self-exploration for yourself, how can you ask your client to take the journey? The "do as I say, not as I do" perspective immediately causes the client to distrust the process and sometimes even the therapist. You handicap the power of EMDR before you ever begin.

THE HERO'S FLAW

All heroes have a flaw. These flaws come in many forms. They can be physical flaws, a wound from some battle, or a confrontation with the villain. It can be some emotional weakness, blinded by the lust for power, greed like Ebenezer Scrooge, jealousy, or just incompetence. When you think of someone to save Middle Earth from evil forces who are out to destroy it, you probably will not choose a three-foot Hobbit with big feet. You probably would not choose a five-foot-six-inch comedian with no military experience from Ukraine to save the west from Russia.

This irony is the nature of the hero. You would be hard-pressed to find any movie whose protagonist is not flawed. Protagonists are commonly drunks or recluse detectives whose spirit is broken from the last encounter with a serial killer. They are sometimes the proverbial outsider who is the only one who saves the day. Superman has his Kryptonite. Luke Skywalker lost his hand, a wound by his father. Achilles, the great warrior, had only one weak point—his heel.

Most of our clients have a diagnosis, and their flaws are evident. The EMDR therapist is looking for THE flaw, which is not hard to discover. Our client's flaw is their negative core belief. This belief defines their wound(s) and gives us a map for the journey. It's good to remember that flaws are a heroic quality, as is avoidance. All heroes have that flaw, that sacred wound.

CHAPTER 4
THE ADVENTURE BEGINS
THE HERO DEPARTS THE ORDINARY WORLD

Once the EMDR process begins, the hero engages in the adventure. The client has surrendered. When they agree to start EMDR therapy, they have *surrendered* (stage two) and are willing to *cross the threshold* (Hero Step Five). They are ready to begin the journey.

This first session is like most meetings with any mental health provider. There is history-gathering, explaining the process of EMDR, informed consent, and other housekeeping requirements. For me and my trainee, a request for a timeline is given as homework. This requirement has fallen out of fashion for some clinicians, but for me, the timeline is a magical document that provides the client's negative core belief in its contents. The instruction to the client is simple; they are asked to list in a few words about a dozen distressing events they experienced in their life.

Sometimes they do not know where to begin, so to help them, they are asked to list one or two upsetting memories that their mother caused, their father caused, present or past bosses or teachers caused, and also a few from past romantic relationships or friendship.

This timeline review is the first step in bringing the client out of the ordinary world and into the hero's adventure. Remember, cognition was developed early in life. The timeline addresses different areas of the client's life; the core belief is revealed in many events.

Here are some common items clients list on their timelines with the core belief listed next to each event. All I know about the client is what is on the timeline. While reviewing the timeline, the negative cognitions are not discussed or shared with the client. It might be hard for the client to accept, and now is not the time to discuss negative cognitions. Remember this is usually the second meeting with the client, so the conversation about the reality of the negative cognition might be done in the second session or not until the third session.

Timeline

Told I was adopted. *I don't matter. My biological mother disposed of me.*

Alcoholic parents. *I don't matter. Alcohol did.*

Dad wanted a boy. *I'm not good enough or I'm a disappointment.*

Lost chess tournaments. *I'm not good enough.*

Mom loved Sis, hated me. *I'm not good enough.*

Flunked out of college. *I'm not good enough.*

Dad left for another woman. *I don't matter.*

Husband had an affair. *I'm not good enough.*

Dad's cancer. *I'm not in control.*

Molested by stepdad; mom knew and didn't stop it. *I don't matter.*

Reviewing the timeline tells me the client's negative core belief immediately. It tells me the template needed for the journey and the obstacle that the client will encounter on this hero's journey. For example, if the client is an *I don't matter* person, I know that EMDR will most likely target parents who are selfish, perhaps alcoholic, overly busy, or just uninterested in their child. Early in life, my client received the message that they do not matter. Everyone else does. Their behavior is to do whatever they're told and always put other people's needs ahead of their own.

You can see with minimal information. The negative core belief can be identified. Each of these items can have other cognitions that will fit. For example, a client who reports molestation in their history might think they are trapped or are in danger as the negative cognition, which is correct. These are the narrower cognitions, as we saw on our chart earlier.

But along with those cognitions, *I don't matter* cognition also fits. The fact that a client's mom did nothing to stop abuse could pair with the thought *I can't trust* and the feeling of being worthless. Most of the time, these significant moments in our lives have more than one thought we can pair with during EMDR. For our purposes, we are identifying the transformation cognitions.

In the domain of the *I don't matter* position, the poisonous king forbids dreams. The client is never permitted to say or even imagine what they want in life. After a while, they just think this is the way things are for everyone.

If they live under the reign of this negative cognition, you can see that in these circumstances, there is no creativity, innovation, or passion about anything. The *I don't matter* client is desolate and dead inside. Whatever gifts or talents they possess are buried deep within. It is too painful to look at these talents because there is no way to lift them out into the sunlight.

As the companion to the hero, the therapist must develop

skills and understanding to identify the transformational belief by interpreting the timeline. The hero has already been warned of the dangers and has decided to take on the task. Once the core belief is identified, the therapist must carefully explain the process. The therapist must also assure the client that they know the safest and most effective path to *cross the threshold.*

The more skilled EMDR therapist identifies the transformational cognitions quickly and knows the problematic behaviors the client engages in that must be extinguished. The therapist understands the safest and quickest route from the old self to the new self. Escaping the poisonous king and entering the land of the sacred king is familiar territory for the therapist who knows the inner genius, creativity, and innovation exist. Often for the first time in their life, the client can ask, "What do I want?" They begin to see the world from a different perspective; they start to see that they are good enough. They understand their value cannot and should not come from others but only from themselves. You see how it is impossible to access the inner genius while under the spell of negative cognition.

The hero will need new skills and protection. For this, assertiveness training is required to pair with further clarity and insight into their truth. *I don't matter* people do not know how to set boundaries or even say no. They would never send cold food back while dining at a restaurant. They would say, "Oh, they're probably busy in that kitchen. I'll just eat it cold." These clients must be taught to speak up. The clients who do transformational work must be warned that EMDR will change four things, including every aspect of their life.

Transformational EMDR will cause change:

1. Their view of the world will change.
2. Their view of themselves will change.

3. How they engage the world will change.
4. How they allow the world to engage them will change.

These are no small things, and each one must be navigated with the help of the therapist. This help requires sage-like wisdom, for these changes are enormous.

HERO STEP SIX: TESTS, ALLIES, AND ENEMIES

This part of the EMDR process is where the heavy lifting occurs. This is the dismantling of the old way. This is painful because insight occurs, causing changes in their behavior. Once the EMDR process begins to show clients how often they allowed others to treat them like they didn't matter or weren't good enough, they experience various emotions. Sometimes they feel despair and say, "I wasted my entire life." "How can I be so stupid to let everyone make all the decisions for me in my life?"

They begin to see the world from a different perspective, a proper perspective. Often, they begin to feel angry for the first time. Once this happens, they are ready to get to work and "answer the call." Eventually, there is an adaptive shift. After much work, they feel they are *good enough* or *matter*. This understanding is vital because these adaptive beliefs do not include anyone but the client. The cognition is not *I matter to my husband* or *I'm good enough for my boss*. It is never about anyone but the client. The negative cognition begins and ends with the client. The client is good enough, or the client matters to themselves, and what anyone else thinks is irrelevant. The client knows in their deepest self that they are okay as they are.

TESTS

The tests for the hero do not only occur during the EMDR session, but the change caused in the session creates change out in the world. EMDR resolves emotional distress and creates new insight and understanding along with clarity. Once this happens, the client must change their behavior, which is often easier said than done. A client might now have a new insight that some of their friends are not friends at all. They are people who use our clients. The test is, can they eliminate them from their life by saying no to toxic requests? This challenge is where EMDR can assist— addressing present issues. The focus of the work is more present and future-pronged. Shapiro's three-pronged approach of past, present, and future events must be addressed for the process to be complete. This present and future focus is to strengthen the client's ego so they can stand up for themselves. These new skills take time to develop. Usually, assertiveness training is required, and behavioral strategies to set healthy boundaries are all necessary skills that must be taught.

After the adaptive shift, the client understands that they have no control over anyone else in their life. They cannot make their parents value them. They cannot make a toxic boss stop being toxic and blaming them for things unfairly, but what they can do is know that no matter what anyone thinks, they are good enough, and they matter to themselves. They stop taking inappropriate responsibility for things that are not their fault, and their movement out in the world changes. The client's internal self-worth comes from one place and one place only. It comes from within. After EMDR, the client feels okay in their own skin. These results do not come in the way of a temporary motivational pep talk. They are permanent and cannot be undone.

These clients walk differently, talk differently, and behave differently. They have a grounded, solid feel about themselves. It sounds like a lame statement to say they are just "okay," but when you think about it, no one is okay. Still, the EMDR client who has traveled the hero's journey is okay and accepting of themselves, unencumbered by anyone else's comments or views. This shift to the authentic self is a powerful and peaceful place to be. They have found their holy grail, their grail castle.

From this new position, the spell of the negative cognition has been broken. Here the client is in the *tests, allies, and enemies* step of the transformation process. Most people around the client with the new sense of self will become adversaries. The new boundaries established by the client will upset some family and friends. These relationships were developed under the control of the *I don't matter* person, and once that changes, family and friends will often not accept the new boundaries and expectations set by the client. The friend and family usually do the following:

1. They try to sabotage the change.
2. They completely reject the person and the family becomes estranged.
3. They will accept the client back into the fold but only if they go back to the old way.

The minute the client sets up healthy boundaries and is no longer available to give everyone everything they want, these relationships fall away. This loss of relationships is not easy. It is sometimes the most challenging part of the journey. A client with this new perspective often relocates, gets divorced, or breaks up with a romantic interest because, in the past, they married or got involved with people who treated them like they don't matter. Once the adaptive shift happens, this can no longer be tolerated. They often quit their job as they search for their authentic purpose because often, they find themselves in jobs their parents chose for them, or the work is unfulfilling, where they are taken advantage of by an abusive boss.

Again, Prince Harry is a visible example of the power of trans-formational EMDR. As we have said, he is an archetypal cultural figure and an *I don't matter* person. He got married, quit his job, left his country, and is estranged from his family in search of his truth. If you think Harry is happy, I think you are mistaken, but whatever distress he feels is endurable because he knows it is in the service of his truth and no one else's. Your clients will do the same thing, although probably in a less visible way. It is still diffi-cult and scary for them. Therefore, ongoing informed consent is necessary. You must warn your client of this dramatic change that may occur. Sometimes this is too much for the client to accept, and the right decision is to leave well enough alone. Therefore, it is necessary to remind clients that EMDR will not give them what they want. EMDR shows the client what is true. This truth is usually quite painful. This transformational work solves the initial set of problems but creates an entirely new set of issues that must be navigated.

They must be aware that old relationships will die, but new healthy relationships will be built from the new *I matter* perspec-tive. They will learn to identify people who truly value them and jettison the rest from their life.

It is not hard to get rid of these people because as soon as you start saying no, they aren't interested in being associated with these heroic clients. They all fall away in short order. The client will move away from these enemies, these allies of the poisonous king, and begin to build healthy friendships as they move toward the land of the sacred king.

HERO STEP SEVEN: APPROACH TO THE INNERMOST CAVE, A TIME FOR CREATIVE INTROVERSION

Transformational EMDR Stage Four: Chaos and Confusion

As one shifts from the old self to the new self, there is a period of chaos and confusion that begins to set in. The client has lost their identity. This period feels like being in limbo, which makes perfect emotional sense for two reasons. First, the client gains insight into the old way of thinking. They see the damage living from the negative cognition's perspective has caused. They know they cannot go back to letting other people take advantage of them or tell them how to live their lives.

The second problem is they do not know how to behave in a world where they have value and have to decide things for themselves. They have no idea what they want or who they are supposed to be. They have no idea how to behave as a person with value. They are in limbo, lost between two worlds. They cannot go back, but they have no idea how to go forward, hence the state of confusion. During this period, it is not uncommon for the client to try and return to their old behaviors and relationships. They soon find that they cannot return to the old way because they have insight and know they are often taken advantage of by others. When they experience this after EMDR therapy, it is intolerable. The therapist should not be alarmed at setbacks because they are not setbacks. They are just part of the process.

This time of in-between is an excruciating time. It is no small thing to lose one's identity. Jung calls this a period of creative introversion. Here the client must do serious introspection to discover the next chapter in their life. No one can tell them what that will be. What does this have to do with the innermost cave?

During the period of chaos and confusion, before the client understands what they want to do with their life, they must move inward and encounter their inner self. Jungians call this a period of creative introversion. Here the client must spend time in solitude journaling, meditating, working with dreams, and continuing with EMDR.

You can see a glimpse of this creative introversion in the epigrams below. Here are three short epigrams written by a person during their struggle in the loss of identity stage of chaos and confusion. These are clearly the words of someone who is being creative and working alone to try and understand where they are in the midst of their quest to find their true self.

Three Epigrams From Hell

I

I do not want your holy water,
nor do I want your sacred bread.
You are not the only one
who has no place
to rest his head.

II

Once exposed to the edge
The fear of
falling ...

never subsides.

III

When the father decides
to purge your soul.

It may take a week.
It may take a year.
It may take the rest of your life,
to get your soul clear.

IN THIS DIFFICULT STAGE, the therapist can help with behavioral skills and more EMDR sessions that are present-focused. They can teach clients the value of dream work, journaling, the need for contemplation and inner exploration. The therapist can help them with assertive skills, and EMDR can continue to strengthen their resolve, but the client must decide what they want to do with their life.

Those who do not stop to contemplate and stay busy distracting themselves from their reality often get hurt or sick in a way that causes them to become temporarily infirm. The unconscious will attack in a severe way. This is not a joke. The unconscious's view: "If you are not going to fulfill your purpose, you might as well be dead."

I can list at least a dozen clients who tried to avoid this work by staying busy and distracted. They either fell, breaking a bone, or twisted a body part that caused them to be immobile for a while. More than one client has had a small stroke. It was not devastating but enough where they had to stop the distractions and convalesce.

I resisted a change in my life in 2018 and ended up in the hospital because my liver stopped working. Literally, I was orange. After four days and a multitude of tests, including a liver biopsy—if you ever get the chance, I'd skip that experience—they found nothing wrong with me.

My liver started to improve with no treatment. The only treatment I received in those four days was one bag of saline. The side effect was two months of fatigue. Apparently if your liver goes crazy, it takes months of rest to repair it. Just for the record, fatigue is not being tired. Fatigue is not having the energy to roll over in bed or needing help going to the bathroom. It is close to being dead. During these two months, I had a lot of time to think and understand what the next chapter of my life was going to be, and I made the change.

As stated earlier, Jung says dreams and the unconscious are not moral. They are amoral. The unconscious will bring you to the edge of death if that is required. The unconscious will do its part to bring you to your true purpose.

This is often the most difficult time for the client. They frequently have no idea where to start this journey inward, because they have no idea what they want. It is at this time Laurie Beth Jones's book is recommended. It is called *The Path*.

The book starts out teaching the client how to write their own life's mission statement and then their vision statement. The way Jones sets up this exercise is brilliant. First, she has pages and pages of words.

You are asked to circle the words you like. Then you must limit your choices to three. When you review the list, you realize that there are more robust words and less robust words, so you choose the most powerful words that describe your mission. The second exercise is to create a vision statement. She asks that this vision statement be written in the first-person present tense. It has to be very specific, not some vague things like "One day I hope to be happy and rich." That won't cut it.[1]

The approach to the inner cave should consist of inner work

like dream work and journaling about what you have lost by living from the maladaptive position and what your hope is for the new perspective. The mission statement is important to do, but the vision statement needs time to figure out. Below is my mission and vision statement when I was in a state of confusion about my life. This was written before I ever thought I would attend graduate school to pursue psychology. I was working in some other businesses at the time and was miserable and failing. For me, dream work was always part of my life, so inner exploration was already in place. I just never dreamed I was smart enough to get into graduate school because I was never a very good student. I had not been in school in twenty years. Setting all these obstacles aside, I wrote my mission and vision.

My Mission is to teach, help and heal with love, compassion, and integrity.

My vision was written in first person with very specific dreams.

I am a psychologist in a successful private practice in Florida. I can see palm trees from the window in my office, and I am a best-selling author. My wife and family are happy pursing their dreams with me.

I wrote these out of a place of despair and being completely confused about my life. I too felt like I had just wasted years of my life when I wrote these words. The values of these exercises are twofold. First, the mission tells you a lot about who you are as a person and what you value and are excited by. The second provides a destination. Once you know what you want, you can set out and get it. It took me ten years, but I got there.

HERO STEP EIGHT: THE SUPREME ORDEAL

EMDR Stages Three and Four: Finding the New Way (resisting the retreat)

DURING THE TRANSFORMATION PROCESS, there are two Supreme Ordeals. Sometimes clients experience one, and sometimes they must deal with both. First, if someone has been chronically abused or neglected as a child, there are multitudes of horrors that clients experienced. Most of the time, they say things like, "That was a long time ago. That doesn't bother me anymore." Sometimes they say, "I worked on that with my previous therapist, so I don't need to talk about that issue."

Asking the client to go back into that memory is a supreme ordeal. Sometimes the historic work is not as bad as the loss of identity in the stage four we just talked about, but it can be. This supreme ordeal can be the worst trauma the clients have experienced. Being sex-trafficked or abused by a family member is some of the worst trauma a person can experience. With EMDR, the client is asked to revisit these memories to process and be free of them. This healing process can be the hero's supreme ordeal, and great care needs to be taken before, during, and after each session.

Then there is the chronic criticism or being parentified by the parents. The child becomes the adult while the parents are self-absorbed in their life or they are alcoholic, workaholics or partiers. The parents can also have mental health issues, which cause the child to realize quickly they have to take care of themselves because the parents are incapable of caring for them. You know—the child who is six years old and is bathing her little brother, who is two. These kinds of childhoods give birth to our two negative cognitions. The parentified child becomes the *I don't matter* person, and the chronically criticized child becomes the *I'm not good enough* child. For these two groups, dismantling the negative belief and accepting the reality of the new belief is the supreme ordeal.

Each client has lived their own life with their own unique experience. The supreme ordeal can be an infinite number of traumatic experiences. In this business, once you think you have heard it all, someone comes in with an even more horrific history than the last. In my previous book, some of these severe cases are discussed, if you are interested. The supreme ordeal is never difficult to identify. It is usually known at the beginning of the work. This is true in mythology; it does not take long for the antagonist to appear as they deliver their evil upon the innocent. So it is in therapy when we ask, "Tell me about your childhood," because that is where we are all vulnerable, and damage is easily perpetrated upon the innocent child.

In this stage of the work, we are dismantling the negative core belief. We are killing the old self, which often causes the client to have nightmares at this initial stage of the process. There is a lot of death and destruction around. Clients have reported being chased by zombies and seeing dead bodies or being stuck in a house that is burning down. Sometimes the client is stranded in a terrible storm with no safe port on the horizon. We are in destruction mode. We are killing the old self, and our inner dreamer will reflect this. It is essential to inform the client of this reality to normalize it. If you do not warn them, they may consider stopping EMDR out of fear of what is happening within them. This happens quite often if the client is not warned about the likelihood of nightmares. Inform them that it is temporary, and it is actually a good thing. It shows we are destroying the unhealthy, maladaptive self.

HERO STEP NINE: REWARD, SEIZING THE SWORD

EMDR Stage Five: Adaptive Change Begins Intrapersonally and Interpersonally

ONCE THE CLIENT has begun to make the adaptive change, as they begin to slowly accept the new perspective and the new life, positive experiences and insights begin to happen. In my thirties, when I was struggling with my life's purpose and my own authentic purpose, I wrote a lot of poetry. Not looking to be a poet but something needed to find its way out. This is truly a period of creative introversion. I have no artistic talent like painting or drawing, but anyone can write a poem. This poem was the last one I wrote. It was at the end of my nine months of depression and figuring out what the rest of my life was going to be. The poem begins by describing a dream I had twelve years prior as a kind of warning of what was going to befall me. During this time, I was not a psychologist. I was a musician and had a failing real estate business. You know, like Jung said, doing my forty years of research.

With no awareness of the steps of the hero and with no knowledge of EMDR, this poem emerged out of my journey, with the steps of the hero identified now in retrospect. When I wrote it, I knew nothing about the hero's journey. This poem expresses the journey beautifully. I needed a mythology to get through this period, and I was able to find it. Let's examine what I wrote. It should be noted that I began journaling and working with my dreams in 1978. I am so glad that internal process was in place. This poem was written twelve years after I recorded that first dream. It's called *The Gift* because the ordeal was a paralyzing, lifesaving and life-changing gift.

The Gift

I have seen the dead, **(ordinary world)**
only once in my life.
Alive he came to me
a dozen years ago.

He brought a gift,
wondrous and mysterious.
It was a fiery sword.
Arthur's heavenly blade.

He drew it from the copper sheath,
held it forward and high.
A great wind blew us back and
Its fire lit up our faces.

He handed it to me but
I could hardly keep it in my grasp.
It took both hands and all of my strength,
this gift from some god.
He said but one phrase in his godlike voice.
Looking me in the eyes,
he spoke slow and clear.
"You are going to need this, my son." **(the call)**

But I had no need of this gift granted me.
I knew not what to do with this heavenly blade.
So, I locked it up in an old oak box,
And the gift became a memory,
Distant and lost. **(refusal of the call)**

Now many years later
this memory becomes alive.
For I have been wounded. **(wound)**
Wounded in a bloody battle
My Holy War. **(the ordeal)**

I felt the old oak box beckon,
I remembered the gift.

I unlocked it.
I could feel it.
The power still vibrant,
I opened it. **(acceptance of the call)**

I held the golden sheath.
Drew the sword with one hand.
No struggle this time to hold it fast.
I understood it.

For
I am a Warrior:
Soul alert.
Accepting no shame
Fearing no swordsman
Enduring my pain.
Fighting my battle,
My Holy Campaign. **(seizing the sword)**

Yes, I am a warrior,
and I will honor only one thing ...

My King. **(Rebirth—returning with the elixir)**

Here the writing clearly begins with the poet avoiding the path. "No thanks. I have no idea what to do with this sword." Then a dozen years later, he endures a wound. He experiences an ordeal and accepts the call after trying to initially refuse the call. The calamity ends ordinary time, and avoidance gives way to surrender. He must take up the cause—seizes the sword. He understands.

By the end, he accepts his new reality. His king—his adaptive shift to the positive thought, *I matter, I am good enough*—is assimilated into his soul. He accepts his new authentic path and is willing to fend off any problems in that process, for he fears no swordsman.

HERO STEP TEN: THE ROAD BACK

Transformational EMDR Stage Five: Seeing Ordinary Life with the New Perspective

As THE CLIENT begins to accept that they have value, they make adaptive adjustments in every area of their life. As we discussed, this can look like jettisoning toxic people from their lives while slowly creating healthy relationships with others. They begin to set healthy boundaries with others, including their family and spouses. They begin to reenter ordinary life; however, it has changed significantly. It's not a life encumbered by their past, where the toxic influence of others interfered, keeping them from their true purpose. Each moment is just about the present moment. The client now has permission to first ask, "What do I want?" They ask this without guilt or entitlement but from a position of their truth and authenticity.

In the EMDR community, at the beginning of the process, we

say, *It is never about now.* In other words, whatever the problem is at that first meeting is not the problem but a symptom of the client's history. The cause of the problem is found in the past. The present problem is just a clue to the cause. So we know it is never about now. The present issue is just a trigger to the connective psychological tissue of the past, where the negative energy of the past is stored. This is easily visible in clients who make a mountain out of a molehill, demonstrating this reality. When this happens, it is clear this client will benefit from EMDR.

We use the same phrase at the beginning of EMDR therapy. We tell the client *it's never about now.* There is a problem happening in the client's present life, but the cause of the problem started in the past. There's another phrase EMDR therapists use to identify the problem that goes along with *it's never about now;* that is PAST is PRESENT. An example of past being present is when a veteran is maybe getting gasoline and he smells diesel fuel. This can cause a flashback. When he experiences this flashback—PAST is PRESENT for him. EMDR corrects this so the past no longer interferes with our clients. This happens to all of us, although usually to a lesser degree than a veteran who has seen combat. We usually are triggered by something that logically is inconsequential, but for some unknown reason, we cannot seem to shake it.

Recently, a client arrived for her session. She was visibly upset because a man cut her off on her way to my office. This sort of thing frequently happens to all of us. It will make most of us angry, but we will soon get over it and move on with our day. She could not get over it. Her negative core belief is *I don't matter.* When this man cut her off in traffic, he caused the energy from all the times in her life when she was treated like she didn't matter to come alive. This is the nature of unconscious memory. We do not get the context or the reason why. We get the emotion and body sensations associated with the history for the thought *I don't matter,* and we usually have no idea why we feel so overwhelmed.

When our client returns to *Ordinary Time,* the past is no longer present. Everything has changed. The new state is calm and peaceful. The moment is just about the moment. All connections to the past have been cut. When this happens, most situations are easy to manage and understand. In this calmness, the client can be excited and passionate about the next chapter in their life, driven by authenticity and their true purpose. The return to the ordinary world often feels uncomfortable because although some things are familiar, many things that look the same are seen in an entirely different light.

Perhaps T.S. Elliot describes this best in four lines in "Little Gidding":

> *We shall not cease from exploration*
> *And the end of all our exploring*
> *Will be to arrive where we started*
> *And know the place for the first time.*[2]

HERO STEP ELEVEN: RESURRECTION

EMDR Stage Five: Rebirth

THIS SIX-STAGE PROCESS is a death and rebirth sequence that our client will travel. The hero's resurrection, their rebirth, is a return from the dead. For the EMDR therapist, this is the beginning of the end of the negative core belief. The chaos and confusion stage is over, and the new cognition is accepted and experienced in the world. With EMDR, there are two stages to the process. In the session, we cause a shift in our thinking. The shift to the adaptive *I do matter* causes a death and rebirth sequence.

The rebirth period is tenuous. Often the client goes back to the old way. They return to the toxic relationship or give in to a boundary set by someone else to make ridiculous requests seem reasonable. Almost without exception, there is an attempt to return to the old way. The client cannot stay there because they see things from the true perspective. Usually, this retreat does not last long for this reason. During this rebirth stage, the client often has dreams of springtime or Christmas. Even if they are atheists, Christmas images occur. It represents the birth of the new way. The inner sacred king is alive within the client. Often small children and toddlers might be in the dream or innocent baby animals. The client is like a baby moving around in this world with this new perspective. They have to find their way. They are not yet steady on their feet, and the dream will reflect this.

HERO STEP TWELVE: RETURN WITH THE ELIXIR

EMDR Stage Six: Assimilation of the New Way

STAGE SIX, assimilation, is the client fully accepting their new reality. There is no longer a need to return to the old way. In fact, the client hardly remembers the old self at all. The new authentic self is accepted; it is engaging the world and others. The new authentic self has been assimilated into the person, and their life is now moving from a position of the positive cognition of self-value and true purpose. The people walk differently, talk differently, eat and sleep differently. Everything comes from their inner sense of authenticity and true purpose. Perhaps Charles Bukowski describes these people best when he says, "the free soul is rare, but you know it when you see it—basically because you feel good, very good, when you are near or with them."[3]

This is where therapy usually ends. For now, the hero's journey has come to a close, but most of us end up with more than one heroic adventure that awaits us, so we are advised to keep our metaphoric hero's sword close. The client is told that life happens even when you have a healthy perspective on yourself and the world. The client is reminded how effective EMDR was for them and that they should return if they encounter any trouble. Usually, they are told to remember the mountain out of a molehill metaphor. If something happens that they can't really shake, they should return for a session or two to alleviate the issue. Remind them that triggers that cause such an experience are linked to the past, and EMDR is the best way to resolve them. This "tweaking" from time to time is necessary and easy to do.

Part Two

SELF-HEALING AND THE SIX STAGES OF TRANSFORMATIONAL EMDR

Shapiro and Jungian Parallels

CHAPTER 5
SELF-HEALING
THE FORGOTTEN ESSENCE OF EMDR
THERAPY AND JUNGIAN PSYCHOLOGY

As we explore the EMDR experience through the eyes of the hero, remember that this works best if the therapist and client are in "flow," which is necessary for *self-healing*. The therapist's primary task is to create the environment for flow to exist. Only within the context of flow can the inner genius in both client and therapist be accessed. Let's take an in-depth look at what Jung and Shapiro say about self-healing, continuing our exploration into our mythic and evidence-based perspective of EMDR.

Self-healing is perhaps the most essential and potent component of EMDR therapy. Self-healing gets a lot of lip service but little commitment to treatment. Shapiro was keenly aware of the importance of committing to the self-healing power of EMDR, as she mentioned it approximately thirty times in her seminal text, *Eye Movement Desensitization and Reprocessing Therapy: Basic Principles, Protocols, and Procedures.*[1]

There are a few challenges when trying to commit to the self-healing element of EMDR therapy. First, the therapist must be patient, which therapists are not usually trained to be. Therapists are trained to intervene. We have these things called interventions, and by their very nature, they are designed to interrupt the client in the service of helping. This approach is the opposite of self-healing. This method of working extinguishes any chance for self-healing to occur. The answer is never found within the therapist. The lack of utilization of self-healing is why you hear people say they have been in therapy for twenty years. The therapist is trying to supply the answer, and the answer is not there.

With EMDR, the therapist has no such role unless there is a problem with the self-healing component of the process. Shapiro asks the therapists to stay out of the way. She frequently states that any intervention, when not needed, interrupts or completely shuts down the EMDR self-healing process. Shapiro never described what happens during EMDR as the Csikszentmihalyi process of flow. She adamantly protected the self-healing process from the over-functioning therapist. She did not want unnecessary interruptions to occur. We know distractions and interruptions end flow. Shapiro also knew the answer was within the client and not the therapist. This "hands off" idea is often lost in recent days. Therapists have gotten in the habit of interfering when there is no need to do anything except wait, watch and listen.

> "Because of EMDR therapy's emphasis on *self-healing,* any premature attempt by the therapist to intervene may slow or stop the client's information process" (Shapiro, 2018, 37).

Once flow is interrupted, it is destroyed and sometimes irretrievably for that session. We will talk later about how to intervene, when necessary, without interrupting flow.

Shapiro continues,

"The Adaptive Information Processing Model is a concept of psychological *self-healing*, a construct based on the body's healing response to injury" (Shapiro, 2018, 28, 37, 43).

Some additional examples of her encouraging the self-healing process by protecting flow are below when she says:

"Resolution of the disturbance is achieved through the stimulation of the client's inherent *self-healing* processes" (Shapiro, 2018, 43).

"EMDR therapy is a client-centered approach in which the clinician acts as a facilitator of the client's own *self-healing* process" (Shapiro, 2018, 135).

"The integrative AIP model underscores a methodology that stimulates the presumed *self-healing* mode of an inherent information processing system" (Shapiro, 2018, 24).

"I regard this healing process as an activation of a person's innate ability to heal psychologically just as his body heals itself when he is physically wounded. A *self-healing* system like this makes sense" (Shapiro, 2016, 18).

"The important thing to remember is that it is your own brain that will be doing the healing" (Shapiro, 2018, 191).

Despite Shapiro's emphasis on the self-healing nature of EMDR, all of her imploring EMDR therapists to stay out of the way often goes unheeded.

Jung thought similarly but wrote in a more poetic voice about the self-healing nature of psychoanalytic work. He expresses the same "self-healing" idea below:

"The way is within us, but not in gods, nor in teachings or in laws" (Jung, 2012, 231b).

"We must dissolve matter *in its own water* thus setting into motion profound and mysterious happenings within" (Edinger, 1993, 1).

In his biography, Jung ascribes his change in thinking to a hands-off approach, much like what EMDR therapists employ, where he began trusting the self-healing aspect of psychoanalysis. Jung stated, "I felt it necessary to develop a new attitude toward my patients. I resolved for the present not to bring any theoretical premises to bear upon them but to wait and see what they would tell of their own accord. My aim became to leave things to chance. The result was that the patients would spontaneously report their dreams and fantasies to me. I would merely ask, 'What occurs to you in connection with that or how do you mean that, or where does that come from? What do you think about it?' The interpretations seemed to follow of their own accord from the patients' replies and associations."[2]

Jung's new hands-off query is precisely what we ask during the EMDR processing query. We say, "What are you noticing?" That's it. And Jung similarly asks, "What occurs to you in connection to that?" Jung and Shapiro both embrace this hands-off psychoanalytic approach to access the self-healing aspect of the psyche, thus keeping the client in flow.

The problem is that when a client is in flow, the therapist interrupts, and any question that does not enhance flow destroys flow. An open-ended question like, "What are you noticing?"

keeps the client in the moment. It keeps them exploring within. A question like, "Where do you feel that emotion in your body?" destroys flow. When the therapist asks such a question, the client now has to go to the thinking part of their brain to answer the unnecessary, flow-destroying questions. The client searches for a body sensation and tries to please the therapist by answering this question, which kills the flow state. At this point, the client might be able to get back into flow, but it may take a few sets. This destruction of flow damages the client because it extends the time they must experience Phase Four, the most distressing phase of the therapy, because of these unnecessary questions. It also lengthens the session overall. If you ask unnecessary questions frequently during a session, you may not even get to the adaptive shift of Phase Five—this problem is remedied by stopping unnecessary questions that interrupt flow.

If the body were the most salient thing the client was experiencing, then they would say so. If the emotion is the most salient thing and you ask them about something else, like where do you feel that emotion in your body, the client goes right to their frontal lobe and tries to answer the question you just asked. This question immediately takes the client out of flow. You might as well ask them what they plan to eat for dinner. The effect is the same. It destroys flow. These unnecessary questions cause unneeded pain and suffering for the client.

You can get decent results with EMDR if you ask unnecessary questions. EMDR almost always works at some level, but the results are much less robust than those achieved by a skilled therapist who creates flow.

The second problem newly trained EMDR therapists confront is their discomfort with the idea of not knowing. As therapists, we are supposed to know. Therapists are taught to know stuff—a lot of stuff. "I'm the therapist. I am supposed to know." We went to school to know. Now the self-healing aspect of the work turns that premise on its head, and we must accept that we do not know. To work from an "I don't know" perspective requires relearning new skills and forgetting old ones. The results will be modest if the therapist cannot surrender to the process, just like we ask the client to do.

Patience is a necessary ingredient for excellent EMDR work to occur. Waiting patiently for this unknown thing to manifest in the process is challenging and new to most therapists. The solution to the problem is within the client. This aspect of self-healing creates some anxiety for the therapist, and to relieve their discomfort, they interfere, which satisfies the therapist's discomfort but leaves the client where they began, looking for the answer.

The reality is that allowing oneself to not know opens the door for the inner genius to appear. This creative inner wisdom can only be accessed in the land of not knowing, where the instruction is simply to *wait, watch and listen.* "Only in silence can you hear the word."

Jungian analyst and author Robert A. Johnson reinforces this idea of the power of *not knowing* below:

I find that things work out best when I remind myself that I do not know (Johnson, 1998, 81).

Sanford warns,

If the therapist adopts a superior attitude toward his client and acts in a godlike know-it-all way, they will keep the client in an inferior, ill position. All health to the therapist and all illness to the patient. If the therapist is well and the client sick, the therapist will not be able to understand that the answer is within the client and not within the all-knowing healthy therapist (Sanford, 1977, 33).

The danger that Sanford warns of is prevented by acknowledging and accepting *self-healing* as the foundation for the way back to health. If the therapist must be all health and the patient all illness, the therapist is working under the domain of the poisonous king.

Accepting that "not knowing" is in the service of self-healing begins to set the stage for flow, creating the environment for the therapist to stop thinking and just wait, watch, and listen. If they wait for the Kairos Moment, that stroke of inner genius emerges from the flow of EMDR.

The third problem for the therapist is that they do not trust that what needs to happen will happen, so they feel uneasy. The way that they soothe themselves is to interfere in the service of trying to help. Unnecessary interference does not help. Unlike Ryan and his Kairos Moment, they have not reached the level of trust to allow themselves just to watch, wait, and listen. Trusting in that self-healing process is daunting and believing that what is needed will show up when they need it is not easy; however, the rewards are great if this skill is developed.

The flow of self-healing exists with EMDR and not many other therapies because EMDR is done in silence. The client is left in their own thoughts to heal. Sometimes an EMDR session is the first time a person has sat quietly and focused on themselves in years, if not decades. The therapist facilitates this solitary process as bilateral stimulation is applied. Jung, too, embraces the solitary approach, using the active imagination strategy he developed that EMDR therapists know as extended resourcing or inner child work that is done by using the imagination in a functionally active way.

Jung did not have access to bilateral stimulation, but he did use the client's imagination, fantasy, and dreams to guide the process. He felt the most relevant information would come from the unconscious, not from the frontal lobe. Shapiro also encourages the processing of images and dream material when appropriate. Shapiro and Jung recognize the process as a solitary inward mindful state of "self-healing." Mihaly Csikszentmihalyi would call this flow.

Shapiro's notion of the self-healing process and Jung's alchemical examination of this internal process are congruent. Both models promote the idea that the solution is within the client and the therapists should be reluctant to interfere.

CHAPTER 6
SIX STAGES OF TRANSFORMATION
JUNG AND SHAPIRO: OVERVIEW OF THE SIX-STAGE MODEL

S ince we are exploring how to hold mythic space in an evidence-based world, we will examine components shared by both models, Jung's mythological view and Shapiro's evidence-based view. First, we will explore the similarities between these two models. Second, there is a six-stage mythic process, the hero's journey that the clients move through when EMDR is used as a transformational process and not simply a way to remove symptoms. We will explore these six stages in the context of these two perspectives.

Once the parallels between these two models are explained and understood, the Jungian lexicon and transformational stages will be examined in the context of the Eight Phases of EMDR Therapy. Shapiro states that "integrating models with EMDR causes profound psychological change" (Shapiro, 2018, 52). By the end of this book, you will understand how to create profound psychological change.

Shapiro always encouraged integrating EMDR with other

models, stating, "All of the salient elements of the primary psychological modalities, as well as the indicators of profound psychological change, will be apparent in an integrated EMDR therapy approach" (Shapiro, 2018, 52). Additionally, she edited the text *EMDR as an Integrative Psychotherapy Approach,* where she states,

> The clinician's mind must be open to the fact that rapid, profound, and multidimensional change occurs and is maintained over time. For those clinicians trained in a long-term model such as psychoanalysis, this may be difficult to accept. However, let me stress that clinical observations of EMDR processing sessions have revealed that no pertinent state of healing is skipped. Symbols become clear, insights occur, lessons are learned, and the various stages of emotional resolution are experienced, albeit in an accelerated fashion.[1]

A counterpoint to Shapiro's request that the psychoanalytic therapist accepts the accelerated nature of EMDR therapy is for the EMDR therapist to keep an open mind about the power of Jungian integration with EMDR. Jungian analyst and writer the late Edward Edinger states,

> The process of psychotherapy, when it goes at all deep, sets into motion profound and mysterious happenings. It is possible for both patients and therapists to lose their way. Therefore, narrow and inadequate theories of the psyche are clung to so desperately—at least, they provide some sense of orientation. We must seek categories for understanding the psyche within the psyche itself and not from some preconceived and often inadequate theory.[2]

Shapiro also warns of inadequate models, as she always encourages integrating EMDR with other models to heed Edinger's warning of clinging to narrow and inadequate theories. One thing about EMDR, it is not narrow or inadequate. EMDR is a lightning bolt that moves through a client's entire life at the speed of thought.

This advanced way of thinking informs the clinician how robust the process can be when unifying both models because it dramatically enhances generalization, causing further acceleration of the EMDR process. Understanding this process from not only a psychological process but a mythic process and even a spiritual process creates an incredible richness of profound meaning as they take up this journey toward their true self.

Although the EMDR process uses psychoanalytic elements, Jungian depth psychology has all but been omitted from the discussion, and so has his mythic view of the work. There are no EMDR myths, and the hero is nothing more than the sick patient. EMDR exists only in a world where the patient must be ill and have a diagnosis. The idea of a mythic pattern being present during EMDR is not evidence-based and is mainly excluded from the EMDR therapy conversation.

We will now discover just how much of EMDR therapy is Jungian. The first part of this book showed us that the myth of the hero and inner genius easily integrates into the evidence-based world of EMDR. The integration of these models and a new way of thinking about the EMDR process dramatically enhance its power. This integration is not trying to put a round peg in a square hole. EMDR is, at its core, a psychoanalytic process (Leeds, 2016). During the evolution from EMD to EMDR (Shapiro, 1991), Shapiro thought the mechanism of action at work during her early understanding of the eye movement process was related to prolonged exposure. By 1995, however, she incorporated the principle of free association as the mechanism at work during "repro-cessing" and not simply desensitization. This realization caused Shapiro to change the name from EMD to EMDR. She observed reprocessing as *free association; therefore, the psychoanalytic model was embraced* as she moved away from an *exposure model* of EMD.[3]

The relevance of this psychoanalytic influence within EMDR has been lost or limited to the free-association component. We will see, however, that psychoanalytic material manifests throughout the eight phases of EMDR therapy. This robust material is unnoticed and, therefore, not utilized. Despite Shapiro's statement that clinicians who use a psychodynamic approach might notice *free association, catharsis, abreaction, symbolism, and family of origin material* (Shapiro, 2018, 49), psychoanalytic characteristics of EMDR are not underutilized but not recognized as psychoanalytic and not understood to be Jungian at its source.

Jungian psychoanalytic thinking integrates everything under the sun. Jung examined mythology, astrology, alchemy, Christianity, Buddhism, Kabbalah, Islam, and Hinduism, as well as empirical data of his time. Integration for Jung was an integral part of his model and his way of thinking. EMDR accesses the collective unconscious, where he believes the wealth of wisdom resides. If the therapist can initiate EMDR and create flow, the portal to this infinite reservoir of knowledge is accessed. It is this access that causes self-healing to occur.

Within the framework of EMDR, we will protect flow for the client and access the inner genius of both the client and therapist. For added power, the therapist will understand this new Jungian language, which will further accelerate the heroic journey that is EMDR.

Another extraordinary factor that occurs when unifying these two models is that within EMDR, processing generalization expands dramatically. We recall from the choice of negative cognitions that the transformational cognitions like *I don't matter* or *I'm not good enough* process more psychological material than *I'm stupid* or *I can't trust my judgment*. When we understand and recognize the Jungian lexicon and hear the language of the unconscious, generalization is further enhanced. This generalization occurs in any of the transformational stages where EMDR is deployed.

Shapiro states that symbols become clear, insights occur, lessons are learned, and the *various stages* of emotional resolution are experienced, albeit in an accelerated fashion (Shapiro, 2018, 46). What stages is Shapiro referencing? It is not clear.

The EMDR therapist understands that the shift from negative to positive cognition is a move from one stage to another, from one perspective to another, and hopefully, from emotional distress to emotional relief.

To understand all six stages of our transformational EMDR process, we need both Jung's and Shapiro's discussions of stages within their perspective models. Each used their own language to describe these stages. Jung describes this multi-stage process as the individuation process. Shapiro understood the process as an adaptive shift that brings permanent relief.

EMDR therapy, as Shapiro has stated, is a clinical process that causes profound and permanent psychological change as it moves through the stages. Shapiro warns that *"insights occur, lessons are learned, and the **various stages of emotional resolution**"* will be experienced in an accelerated manner. By examining their ideas of psychological change, the stages become evident. By examining these two models, we will identify a consistent and predictable map of the transformational process. This process very definitely occurs in discrete stages. These six stages have been written about throughout history in mythology, literature, religions, and film. It is the hero's journey, as we will see as we identify each distinct stage.

Jung calls himself a scientist and respects science but often writes like a writer of literature rather than an academic and warns of the danger of science.

Jung states,

"Science is not, indeed, a perfect instrument, but it is a superior and indispensable one that works harm only when taken as an end in itself ..." [4]

Shapiro respects the psychoanalytic properties of EMDR therapy, utilizing free association, dream material, fantasy, and images. She is, however, very much an empiricist. Integrating both views, scientific and artistic, provides us with incredible therapeutic power that allows us to take this mythic journey in the scientifically sound vessel that is EMDR.

Jung gives an example of empirical inquiry versus artistic and philosophical inquiry. This is a single example that represents what we are doing in a much larger scale. We are trying to see our work globally work from both sides, art and science, while integrating them together. See Jung's thoughts below:

"If one tries to understand a Gothic cathedral under its historical, technical, and mineralogical aspect, this is *a scientific examination*. But where is the meaning of the marvelous edifice? Where is the answer to that all-important question: what goal of redemption did the Gothic man seek in his work, and how have we to understand his work subjectively, in and through ourselves?" [5]

In our exploration, Shapiro provides the science, the historical, technical, and neurological aspects to this powerful process we call EMDR therapy; Jung provides the subjective, mysterious and mythic view of the psychological process of healing and transformation. As Shapiro stated, both models move a client through the therapeutic process using symbols, images, and the various stages of emotional resolution.

CHAPTER 7
AVOIDANCE
TRANSFORMATIONAL EMDR STAGE ONE

The remainder of this section of the book's Part II explores the six stages of transformational EMDR. Just to remind the reader, the six stages are:

1. Avoidance
2. Surrender
3. Dismantling the old self
4. Loss of identity—chaos and confusion
5. Rebirth
6. Assimilation of the new self[1]

We will take each one of these and examine them from an EMDR perspective and the Jungian perspective.

AVOIDANCE

If we return to the story of the Fisher King, Parsifal is our hero, but he is naïve and unaware of his call. He is brought in to see the king but does not ask the question and fails. He is sent away with many other knights who fail. Soon his naivete disappears as he experiences the heaviness and cruelty of the world seeking the grail castle and the cure for the king.

The client from the ordinary world will surrender and set out to answer the question: What is my purpose? Where is my grail castle?

Most clients experience avoidance during the time in the hero's ordinary world. They live through the lens of their negative cognition, the reign of the poisonous king. They survive this desolate world using defense mechanisms like denial, intellectualization, rationalization, etc. They have other more detrimental ways to avoid as well. Other ways to avoid include addiction to alcohol, drugs, pornography, gambling, or less apparent addictions like exercising, overworking, shopping, etc. Humans are brilliantly innovative in ways to avoid reality.

Once the client enters the therapist's office, some of them know they must stop avoiding, but avoidance does not always end because they happen to be in a therapist's office. Breaking through avoidance is often part of the initial EMDR work or therapeutic work in general. The client can enter the office and know they need help. When they are told what is required, they often balk.

Shapiro tells us that "avoidance implies that a person is not willing to self-heal" (Shapiro, 2018). The skilled EMDR therapist expects this refusal. It is not by chance that the first step of the hero's journey is the refusal of the call. Avoidance is natural and very human. Skinner was right. Humans avoid pain and seek pleasure, although, as we have discussed, that is not the entire story.

Jung and Shapiro understood avoidance. Both saw resistance as the fear of the unknown. We humans have many ways to avoid, and we use them effectively. Avoidance is one phenomenon shared by all humans.

The rationale for avoidance is described by Jung, Sanford and Shapiro below:

"The individuation process is usually quite painful. It requires learning much about ourselves we would prefer not to know, and assuming the burden of our inner conflicts. Becoming whole is a dark and dangerous passage and it is small wonder that most people *avoid* it if they can" (Sanford, 1997, 21).

"The opening up of the unconscious always means the outbreak of intense spiritual suffering. This encounter shows just how thin are the walls that separate a well-ordered world from lurking chaos." (Jung, 1969, CW 11, §531)

"Having a relationship with the unconscious is like letting in heaven and hell simultaneously" (Sanford, 1977, 100).

"Encountering the unconscious should only be attempted by psychologically mature individuals who are capable of withstanding a powerful confrontation with the unconscious" (Jung in Chodorow).[2]

"Clients with anxiety disorders, and a history with trauma are likely to display *avoidance* at the outset of treatment" (Shapiro, 2002, 114).

Here Shapiro implies that avoidance happens at the beginning of treatment. It is the beginning of our mythic perspective presented empirically; it is our stage one of the hero's journey. Jesus himself uttered the words at the beginning of the process of his death and resurrection, "Please let this cup pass from me." Clearly, avoidance is where the journey begins. It is the hero's refusal of the call. It is understood psychologically, empirically, spiritually and mythically. Avoidance is not a theory; it is a law of nature as absolute as gravity.

James Hillman agrees with Campbell as he states,

"Symptoms lead to soul (psyche), the cure of symptoms may also cure away soul, get rid of just what is beginning to show, at first tortured and crying for help, comfort, and love, but which is the soul in the neurosis trying to make itself heard, trying to impress the stupid and stubborn mind—that impotent mule which insists on going its unchanging obstinate way."[3] *Stay the course of the poisonous king. (Italics mine)*

As does John Sanford:

"Anything rejected in the unconscious turns against us, *becomes an adversary;* on the other hand, to give conscious energy to the contents of the unconscious is to begin to win their positive energy and support. *Unconscious begins to function as an ally* (Sanford, 1977, 94). (*Italics mine*)

Shapiro tells us that avoidance perpetuates the problem. "It is this avoidance that keeps their problem alive" (Shapiro, 2018, 66). In a sense, the problem is the devil the client knows. There is no clear view of what life without the pain will be like for the client. It is an unknown commodity, and nothing is more terrifying than the unknown. This familiarity with the problem keeps violently abused women with their partners. The violent reality is one they know. It is familiar. People get accustomed to this way of life.

The insidious nature of the negative core belief is that we

create a world for ourselves based on this belief, and although we are unhappy there, we do not know how to live any other way. We become comfortable and attracted to who and whatever perpetuates our negative core belief. Being attracted to and comfortable with those people who take advantage of us or remind us that we are not good enough occurs without the client's awareness. It exists under the radar unconsciously. For example, a woman who does not matter chooses a man who seemingly is kind and caring but turns into a violent, abusive partner. She escapes and learns to be careful with her next partner. She chooses a gentle nonviolent partner and asks him to take out the trash because it is overflowing. He says okay, but he never takes the trash out because she does not matter. These two men are diametrically opposed to one another, yet they are also exactly the same. She tries to choose a better man, but she is attracted to the men who will perpetuate her negative belief of not mattering without her really knowing or understanding why. This pattern is not a gender-specific phenomenon. Men and women both fall victim to their negative cognition.

When the avoidance is strong, and the hero's *refusal of the call* is fixed, extraordinary measures may be required to break through this avoidance.

We are dealing with two potential levels of rejection: the temporary hesitation that is part of every journey and the complete rejection of the call when the client refuses the invitation. The journey denied. Sometimes the unconscious will not tolerate this refusal, and it begins an adversarial relationship with the person. Pathology gets more severe; nightmares and interrupted sleep occur. Things get worse until the person returns out of desperation from increased internal torment.

Although the call is refused, the unconscious will sometimes not be denied. Sometimes this does not happen, and the person does not change or engage in the journey. And sometimes, people never get the call. Millions of people do not get the invitation to become self-aware and authentic. You do not have to look around very far to see those people. If the client is in my office in a state of despair, I tell them how lucky they are to have gotten the call.

A colleague of mine who discussed a dream of one of her clients demonstrates a classic avoidant dream.

> This client is in an auditorium. It is sparsely filled with a few people when someone opens fire and shoots him (the client dreamer). Nothing to worry about as he is wearing a bulletproof vest. "Don't worry. I'm okay." No one can harm him. The dream ended.

For the uninitiated, this might seem like a good dream; he was protected. But it is not. The client has to die for the new self to be born. He is unchanged and unwilling to change. My colleague reported as much in our discussion about this client's situation. This client is in therapy with a great therapist. It is up to him if he will permanently refuse the call or if he will relent and engage the journey.

Recently I had an exchange with a young woman who was complaining to me about the results of the serious EMDR work she had done. She was not my patient but knew I was an EMDR practitioner. Her complaint: After years of EMDR, she found herself content and at peace. She hated it!

She complained, "There is something wrong with me.

"Yesterday, I was at my new job. I went to my first staff meeting. I had prepared material that I thought I needed, but it was the wrong material."

She continued, "Normally, I would have been horrified. I

would have felt ashamed and embarrassed, and I probably would have run out of the place, never to return.

"But that's not what happened. Instead, I was quite calm.

"I apologized, made a few notes of what I need to get for the next day and listened intently to the rest of the meeting and did not give my mistake a second thought."

One might think this is great, right? Not to her. She wanted to go back for therapy to fix this.

I asked her what she would tell her therapist: that she feels calm, peaceful, and content and wants to feel anxious and emotionally fragile again after all her work. After experiencing this dramatic change, still there is an element of avoidance. She wants to go back, but she cannot. She can only go forward. She is experiencing a loss of identity. Her therapist may not have given her adequate warning about just how dramatic the change can be with EMDR therapy. This is why ongoing informed consent is so important. It is important as the therapist to explain this journey to the client before you begin.

If people think it is crazy that a woman in a violent relationship goes back to her violent partner, logically, it is crazy. Still, emotionally, this decision makes perfect sense. Like the woman who was peaceful, calm, and able to handle stressful situations for the first time in her life, she felt something was wrong with her. The hold that the poisonous king has on clients is strong. So with maladaptive behaviors we see all around us or those we even engage in ourselves, they make sense emotionally. Those behaviors are the devil we know. Without them, who would we be?

Letting go of these issues can be challenging because it leaves us with the unknown. Who will I be without being a victim or without my anxiety or panic? Who am I if I am no longer a disabled veteran? The loss of self is a terrifying reality. Clients know it, and as clinicians, we must warn them that this happens with EMDR. EMDR changes things, and the change is permanent. Buyer beware.

As we have explored, avoidance is an authentic thing, and it can be a problem because we have seen the emotionally powerful hold the negative cognition has on the client to maintain the status quo.

Convincing the client to move past avoidance is a challenge. The client must understand the risks and dangers they will face. Fortunately, the EMDR therapist functions as a guide who has assisted many people through this passageway to a new understanding of this unfamiliar terrain on the other side of the new world. With some practice, the clinician can break through avoidance. Avoidance, although problematic, is temporary for those that come to the therapist with a desire to make genuine change.

Shapiro sees the old way that we seek to change through the lens of negative beliefs or cognitions. She explains that a lack of safety results in *avoidance* (Shapiro, 2018, 134) of the work. Avoidance in the EMDR world is avoiding an encounter with the feared stimulus or the negative cognition, whether it's from the past, present, or even fear of something in the future.

As we have said, Freud had an in-depth understanding of avoidance, identifying how humans maintain avoidance through the defense mechanisms he identified. All defensive mechanisms are in the service of avoidance. Defense mechanisms can work for years until the unconscious's adversarial position becomes active. When defense mechanisms fail, pathology occurs. Often this pathology is symbolically meaningful, as we will discover. Depression, anxiety, and panic often occur one day, unexpectedly, and for no apparent reason. Unconscious coercion might be a panic attack or nightmares. Irrational fear about something suddenly attacks the client. These are all caused by the unconscious, which is trying to get your attention to change. You are off course, and the unconscious is providing a navigational adjustment.

Accept and attend to it, and it will assist. It becomes an ally.

> The right reaction to a symptom may as well be a welcoming rather than laments and demands for remedies, for the symptom is the first herald of an awakening psyche which will not tolerate any more abuse. Through the symptom the psyche demands attention. Attention means attending to, tending, a certain tender care of, as well as waiting, pausing, listening. It takes a span of time and a tension of patience. Precisely what each symptom needs is time and tender care and attention (Hillman, 1989, 18).

Below is a powerful example shared by Francine Shapiro that demonstrates the idea of the unconscious as an adversary and then an ally—from a maladaptive world view to an adaptive. This story is from one of the subjects in her very first research study from 1989.

> A subject who had a lifelong history of one or two violent, fearful dreams per week reported that he had a violent dream on the night following EMD treatment, but that on this occasion he had felt no fear and, in the dream, had "ritually bowed to his Samurai enemies." They had then joined forces and he had no subsequent violent or fearful dreams. It was as far as he could remember that he had no nightmares and felt consistently good and confident without breaks (Shapiro, 2018, 10).

The unconscious was trying to get him to deal with his issues for his entire life. To take up the call. The unconscious created the nightmares (unconscious as an adversary). After EMD treatment (attending to the problem), he bowed to his enemies and joined forces with them (the unconscious as an ally).

The unconscious, as an adversary or ally, is not as mysterious as it sounds. If you smoke cigarettes, your body will eventually behave like an adversary. Your health will decline. If you avoid the dentist about a toothache, your tooth will become an adversary and intensify the discomfort until you respond. As Shapiro stated, the unconscious works much like our body; it wants to heal, but if ignored, it will behave much like our body behaves, and things will worsen.

To review, a protracted period of avoidance will eventually cause the unconscious to take an adversarial position that ends the effectiveness of any defense mechanisms that maintain this avoidance. The unconscious does this by creating severe distress. This severe distress causes the client to surrender to an "I'll do anything not to feel this way" position—thus, stage two begins.

Stage one: Avoidance—creates distress and pathology, thus leading to surrender, stage two.

Stage two: Surrender.

CHAPTER 8
SURRENDER
TRANSFORMATIONAL EMDR STAGE TWO

S urrender is a key element to therapy in general but specifically to the process of EMDR. As we said earlier, the instruction to the EMDR client encourages an understanding and willingness to surrender to the process, which is demonstrated in the instructions the client is given below:

> Your job is to be a passive vessel. You do not try to make anything happen; nor do you try to prevent anything from happening. Your job is to stay out of the way and ALLOW whatever is happening to happen. Remember it is your own brain that is doing the healing. EMDR Therapy activates thoughts, feelings, images, memories, and body sensations. Sometimes you may experience all of these things and sometimes you may have a string of thoughts and then a memory and some feelings. You do not need to understand what is going on or remember it. Your job is just to allow whatever is happening to happen.[1]

Heroic myths have the hero accepting the call, or there would not be a story.

As we have said, sometimes this is done by coercion, and sometimes the call is accepted without coercion. As with the myth, so it is with therapy. Some people walk in the door and know something has to change. They need little or no convincing. Others, like my colleague's client, need more encouragement to allow the old self to die to make way for the new self.

When surrender is driven by extreme distress, the defense mechanism that maintains avoidance is usually failing. Ways in which the client has behaved for most of their life are no longer getting the desired result. This often unbearable distress brings the client in for treatment.

The EMDR instruction to "allow" whatever wants to happen is the ultimate surrender instruction. As we have said, the therapist must try to stay out of the way to not interfere with the flow so the client can find flow and allow whatever wants to happen to happen. This process must be done without thinking or having an intention. All of the instructions from Jung and Shapiro come together in the service of self-healing.

Here the ideas we discussed are essential to facilitate surrender. "The therapist should try to allow the processing to continue without undue interference" (Shapiro, 2018, 142). These instructions reinforce the notion that the client can self-heal, and the therapist must allow this self-healing to occur by not interfering. As Jung instructs, "dissolving matter in its own water" sets in motion profound and mysterious happenings (Edinger, 1993, 1); this dissolution process cannot occur until avoidance ends, surrender begins, and the therapist understands that it is the self-healing nature of the process they must facilitate.

The EMDR therapist might assume these instructions are limited to sessions of bilateral stimulation only. As we will see, the assistance that comes from the unconscious helps with dreams, within the talk sessions, and in events that occur daily in a client's life. This self-healing occurs within the client twenty-four seven.

The therapists' overall role is to follow the client, to accept they may not know or understand what is happening and to wait, watch and listen for the language of the unconscious to assist. They must function as a receptor and not the all-knowing therapist.

The client must be willing to accept this ambiguity of knowing and not knowing. Knowing the old way does not work, and they do not know what the new way is or if it will work. This not knowing can cause extreme distress. They must be reassured that this process will work. It might cause short-term distress but eventually leads to long-term gain. It is essential to normalize this reality as the process is described to warn their clients of the distress they may encounter. The EMDR therapist is trained to inform the client in great detail about the journey they are embarking on. The client decides if they are willing to surrender or not. "While the eye movements are going on, don't try. You just need to give feedback on what is happening. *Just let whatever happens, happen*" (Shapiro, 2018, 183).

Some therapists are unaware that they, too, must heed the instruction. Not only does the client have to surrender, but so does the therapist. The therapist must accept what is given. For Shapiro says, "There are no supposed to's in this process. Just let whatever wants to happen to happen" (Shapiro, 2018, 123). This may seem like an instruction solely for the client, but the therapist must also abide by this instruction unless some problem occurs that they need to address.

"Allowing processing to progress unimpeded can be extremely difficult for many clinicians" (Shapiro, 2018, 148).

Here Shapiro implores the therapist to stay out of the way. She states this repeatedly in her text. The therapist must allow the process to play out in every stage.

Clients will often use the word "surrender" during EMDR processing. Sample transcript excerpts from three different clients that state the need to surrender are below:

- "Nothing matters, but objectively I have to do it and I can *surrender* and let God do it."
- "There is no 'there' there. I want to go into the emptiness and *surrender* and let go of the world with only my idea of the world."
- "I let go and *surrender* to a higher will or God comes in a way that my parents never did." (Shapiro, 2002, 332)

"All true things change and only that which changes remains true." (Jung, 1970, CW. vol.11, § 85). This quote implies surrendering to change. Accepting change is required to remain true to yourself. "Do you still not know that the way to truth stands open only to those without intention."[2]

Jung and Shapiro agree that one must surrender to the process, which means you will experience your truth, not what you want, but what is true. Three potential outcomes will occur if a client enters the process with their own agenda:

1. The process will not work if the client does not give up their intention and surrender. They will often end therapy prematurely.

2. If they stop prematurely, often the unconscious creates more distress, and they are compelled to return.
3. They will realize and accept their reality and truth and proceed.

Jung further supports the importance of *the therapist* surrendering to the process. He states, "The therapist must have no fixed ideas as to what is right, nor must he pretend to know what is right and what is not—otherwise, he takes something from the richness of the experience" (Jung, 1969, vol. 11, § 530).

He also states, "Few analysts, and those hardly the most trustworthy, would be prepared to present us with a formula which should cover all the component elements which go into making up an analysis. Just how an analysis will proceed, of what it will consist of, what part in it will be taken by the analyst and what by the patient, what it will and will not achieve, and what paths it will follow: none of these can be determined in advance."[3]

It is clear that both models understand avoidance, surrender, and self-healing to be essential elements of successful therapy and, as we will see, are also components of the hero's journey.

Let's review what we know so far. Both Shapiro and Jung agree that the healing process starts with avoidance, which gives way to surrender. Surrender is a necessary ingredient for self-healing to occur. While all this is happening, there is also an element of "not knowing." The therapist does not know. The client does not know. Within the context of EMDR processing, there is an activation of a transcendent function that reveals what was unknown only moments ago is revealed. As we will see, during EMDR, seemingly unsolvable problems are solved. So we can see the first three parallels of avoidance, surrender, and self-healing are essential in both models.

CHAPTER 9

DISMANTLING OF THE NEGATIVE CORE BELIEF
TRANSFORMATIONAL EMDR STAGE THREE: DEATH OF THE OLD WAY

T he client must be warned of what profound psychological change means and how it might manifest in their life. They must understand that whatever changes occur during EMDR can't be undone. Once you know, you cannot unknow. This warning requires ongoing informed consent. Clients who want to be treated for a single-episode event will usually not move through the transformational process Shapiro describes below.

As Shapiro stated in her 2006 address at the EMDRIA conference, EMDR can provide an entire smorgasbord of choices. Sometimes clients want to eat the whole meal, appetizers, the main course, and dessert (transformational), and sometimes they come simply for an appetizer (single-episode event). The problem occurs when they arrive just wanting to cure a phobia, for example. Still, the process of resolving a phobia has created new insight and a desire to continue working more profoundly. This more profound work usually means dismantling the negative core belief in EMDR. What it means for the client is a complete transformation of their life.

Here, informed consent must be reviewed a second time and should be noted in the record, stating "the client understands the implication of transformational work." This probably did not happen for the acquaintance we discussed earlier who was upset because she was not upset at her new job.

I often instruct my client when the prospect of doing transformational EMDR occurs. I warn them of the change that can occur in the process. This explanation might sound something like this:

If we continue with EMDR, you should understand that EMDR can cause changes in your perceptions. It may change the way you see yourself and the way you see those around you. It can also change the way you engage the world and how you allow the world to engage you. Sometimes these changes can cause tension in relationships or even end relationships. It is essential to know that this often happens because EMDR causes permanent and authentic clarity. You cannot go back to "not knowing," although people usually try. It is essential to know that EMDR will not give you want you want. EMDR will give you what is true. The truth is not always easy to accept. So, I want you to seriously consider these possible changes to make sure you want to do this work. The changes that happen during EMDR cannot be undone. Do you have any questions?

Engaging the hero's journey and creating permanent transformational change is no small thing. The journey to the authentic self resolves one set of problems but creates an entirely new set of problems that must be navigated. These problems are in the service of the true self and are experienced as such. Therefore, they are considered necessary and temporary until the goal is reached.

The goal is to cause the adaptive shift. This shift causes changes in the microcosm (during each session) or macrocosm (out in their world). Jung makes the same case with what he calls the individuation process described below.

"They can no longer live with illusions (the core maladaptive schema), and they can no longer live without letting into consciousness whatever it is that the unconscious wants to bring" (the adaptive core belief/schema) (Sanford, 1977, 33). *Parentheses mine.*

In other words, they must surrender and accept what the process reveals. There are dangers at this point in the process. The dismantling is a shift from the old self to the new self. These changes begin to occur once the negative core belief starts to be dismantled in the processing phases of EMDR. The maladaptive core belief has driven the client's life. EMDR causes it to shift to the adaptive positive belief. One can think of this shift as moving from an "ignorance is bliss" position to the "truth will set you free" position. This truth can be excruciating.

These are quotes from some of my clients as the veil of the maladaptive belief lifts and the true perspective begins: You can see insight, and an experience of the truth is a painful experience. This insight cannot be undone.

"I feel like I've been asleep for twenty years and only now just woke up."

"I feel like my entire life has been a waste. Always doing what others want of me, never asking myself what I want."

"I feel like Rip van Winkle. I've been asleep for forty years."

"Oh, my God. I've been dancing to their tune my entire life."

Our informed consent includes a statement like, "The client must be willing to accept temporary distress for permanent relief" (Shapiro, 2018, 85). As we can see from the client quotes, temporary distress is only half the story. The client must also be willing to accept the permanent, authentic change that may require a long-term adjustment period as the process rids them of illusions and makes conscious what is unconscious, no matter how painful this new insight is for them. Sanford warns of the long-term distress. He describes it as woundedness, and Robert Bly goes a little further, calling it a sacred wound into which the soul enters. The truth is experienced. "Those who enter into the individuation experience are left with a certain woundedness. They can no longer live with illusions, and they can no longer live without letting into consciousness whatever it is that the unconscious wants to bring. Individuation itself is a kind of wound" (Sanford, 1977, 33).

We are implying not only short-term distress but also long-term adjustment. Jung explains that to find ourselves, we must be free from unconscious identification with parents, wife or husband, and children. We cannot fulfill the demands of individuation and authenticity if tribal familial loyalties interfere (Sanford in Dobo, 2015, 66). Shapiro also warns that the EMDR process can create familial and relational problems for the client (Shapiro, 2018, 92).

If we return to our Prince Harry example, it is clear what can happen when the old self is destroyed to make way for the new self. Jung and Shapiro remind us of the cost of changing to the authentic path. Prince Harry is a visible example of the cost. He gave up a kingdom, left his country and family and probably his royal title to courageously seek his authentic purpose. The price is high, but so is the reward. Jung and Shapiro both knew the price of authenticity, and their perspective models have the power to cause permanent and profound change.

I had a Norman Rockwell-like childhood. I was lucky. My

parents often tried to motivate me by comparing me with other kids, which is all a kid needed to hear. These other kids were good enough, and I was not. This motivational effort was not malicious on their part. They were just trying to motivate me ineffectively. My "I'm not good enough" cognition goes back further than that. As I said, I was born prematurely in 1955. On the day I was born I was weak, a disappointment, and I was not good enough.

Usually, we have an early distressing event that solidifies our negative core belief that drives life's perception. I remember when I was in first grade. I misunderstood the instructions for an assignment. When the teacher saw what I had done, she yanked me out of my chair and hit me on my behind a few times and tossed me back in my chair. No one had ever hit me in my life.

Before this event, I liked school; I liked my teachers; I liked my friends. I was a little shy but not afraid until that day. After such an event, everything changed. I realized teachers are dangerous. School can be unpredictable. I better never make a mistake again. I better make sure that my papers look like everyone else's. My worldview changed in that ten seconds. My *I'm not good enough* was reinforced on that day—cemented in my psyche for the rest of my life.

Thirty years later, I ran into an old elementary school friend. We were sharing a beer and started talking about the old days. I did not remember the assignment I was punished for in first grade, but my friend remembered: "You used crayons on your calendar." And then he chuckled, and we laughed about it. He was traumatized by what he saw that day, to the point that he remembered details that I had forgotten. He, too, remembered that he better not make a mistake either. EMDR saved me. If you're interested in that story, you'll have to read my first book, *Unburdening Souls at the Speed of Thought*.

As it is with me, so it is with you. The negative cognition starts as a kid and perpetuates through the lifespan. Clients who endure chronic chaos and violence learn to be quiet and invisible to stay safe. This behavior is resourceful for the child, but being invisible and quiet does not work as an adult. The problem is no one tells you when that day has arrived. It's easy to see how the belief that I am not good enough will affect self-esteem, which will affect mood and can cause pathology. Usually, this is when people come for therapy. They typically do not know why they just had a panic attack or feel depressed, but it was almost without exception that it started with one of the two transformational core beliefs: *I don't matter,* or *I'm not good enough.* We all carry the burden of one or both of those.

Shapiro discusses this transformation process beyond symptom resolution. Once the adaptive shift occurs, the EMDR symptoms are often resolved. Symptom resolution is not the end of the process. Jung and Jungian writers, as well as Shapiro, write about this reality. Jung warns that all psychological transformation requires a period of chaos and confusion. Shapiro warns that the client will have a sense of loss of identity. Shapiro warns that:

> "The EMDR process can result in behavior changes on the part of the client, requiring the clinician to address problems that arise in the family or social system" (Shapiro, 2018, 71).

As previously discussed, but is worth reiterating, family systems tell us that families will interfere with any adaptive change that threatens the family's homeostasis. This interference can cause conflict. Families initially respond in three ways:

1. The family will reject the changing family member.
2. The family will sabotage the change.

3. The family will accept the changing member if they return to their old role.

These things only happen if you are doing transformational work. This deep work is beyond symptom resolution. Let's look at Prince Harry with the three familial responses. Once he gave up his royal duties, the family said, "We aren't paying for your security." "Your daughter will not have a royal title." "Come back and attend to your royal duties, and everything will be forgiven." At this writing, he refuses and is estranged from his family.

Prince Harry is on his hero's journey. Presently he is confused and in a state of chaos and loss of identity. He has no idea who he is or what he is supposed to do. Is he a prince? Is he a celebrity? What is his life's purpose? This is probably the first time in his life that he asked himself what he wants to do. Usually, he was just told what to do, what to say, where to go, and when to be there.

Our clients are not usually princes but will experience these same struggles. Their family and friends will sabotage the change. They will reject them. This includes spouses. It is not uncommon for clients to seek divorce after an adaptive shift.

The insidious nature of the negative core belief is that it is familiar. People marry people who perpetuate the negative belief. If your negative cognition is *I don't matter,* you will marry someone who will treat you like you don't matter. I know this to be true, and it gives me pause. Prince Harry may have married someone to perpetuate his *I don't matter* cognition. Usually, the *I don't matter* person is married to an *I'm not good enough* person. I don't know much about Megan Markel, but she is biracial. Biracial individuals are usually *I'm not good enough* people. Sometimes the *I don't belong* cognition is there too. They don't feel like they belong on either side of the family. They are not white or black, so they don't know where they fit in.

No need to worry too much about Harry and Megan. Remember, 85 percent of all couples have one *I don't matter* person and one *I'm not good enough* person (Johnson, 2005).

Shapiro instructs that the clinician may decide to target new material but should do so only after the previously processed traumas have been completely integrated. In terms of the stages, the integration of traumas Shapiro discusses is the end of our stage three. This method is a cumbersome way to work. This approach is a logical frontal lobe way to approach the process.

Using Shapiro's approach reduces the power of EMDR because this method does not cause significant transformation. This strategy reduces symptoms and is in line with the medical model psychology has fallen prey to. The transformational power of EMDR is to follow the client, follow their unconscious by understanding its language and let it be the guide.

As I said earlier, stop thinking and wait, watch, and listen. There is nothing logical about how the human psyche organizes and expresses itself. Let's say you are working on a sexual assault. The negative belief is often *I'm in danger*, or *I'm not in control*, or *I'm trapped.* It can be any number of these cognitions, but there is also the transformational cognition *I don't matter.* If you mattered at all to this perpetrator, he wouldn't have done this to you. It is not the most obvious cognition, but it is part of this violent event. If the client has that negative cognition as their core belief, it is very difficult to separate the assault from other historic events where that cognition was solidified. It should not be separated. It should be processed.

The transformational understanding shows Shapiro's idea of clearing out targets related to the event is flawed at the outset. If the negative cognition, *I don't matter,* is processed during work on the assault, the client might jump to being ignored by middle school girlfriends when she was just a teen. This is an *I don't matter* moment and is entirely unrelated to the assault. Or is it? This logical way of working reduces generalization and thus limits EMDR's power. A more robust way to work is to wait, watch and listen, then follow the client and the client's unconscious to see where it leads. It usually leads to the right place and the most healing place.

Shapiro says the clinician should not have preconceived plans or agendas, but with this instruction she is doing just that, suggesting a preconceived plan.

There may be times when the client does not want to explore the transformation cognitions and wants her PTSD symptoms to be relieved. In this case, Shapiro's method is useful, but it should not be seen as the only way but as one of two clinical choices: Shapiro's clear-out targets related to the traumatic event, and the other, wait, watch and listen while following the client and their unconscious.

CHAPTER 10
CHAOS AND CONFUSION
TRANSFORMATIONAL EMDR STAGE FOUR:
THE ESSENTIAL INGREDIENT

We understand that these dramatic changes that cause loss of identity usually will cause a client to feel lost about who they are and what they should do. They are in a state of internal chaos and confusion. The old self has to die and the new way discovered. Before the new way is figured out, this in-between stage of confusion occurs. It is the only way for a true psychological transformation to proceed. By understanding the great distress this stage causes for the client, the therapist must give advanced warning to the client.

The loss of identity stage can be the most challenging stage because there is not much the therapist can do to help the client decide what the next chapter of their life might be. They must reinvent themselves, and sometimes they do not know who they are or what they should do. They just know where they are and what they are doing presently is not it. This may be the only thing they know. They know that where they are and what they are doing in their life is all wrong and something has to change.

The effect of this integrative approach turns a client's world upside down. Clients can potentially end family relationships, seek a divorce, quit their job, relocate, and end friendships. Why does this happen?

Moving from the maladaptive perception to adaptive perception is no easy task. Shapiro tells us that "EMDR facilitates profound therapeutic change in much less time than has been traditionally assumed" (Shapiro, 2018, 18). She continues, "Fear of change can be the most difficult of all to address. Fear of success, failure, the unknown, loss of control and especially loss of identity" (Shapiro, 2018, 186). Jung would identify this stage as his chaos and confusion stage, our transformational stage four.

It is the loss-of-identity part of this journey where people say, "I want to stop. I don't want to do any more." But they soon realize once the adaptive shift moves to *I do matter*, they can no longer put everyone ahead of themselves.

Their change in perception and understanding creates enormous problems. Chaos and confusion, loss of identity, are not just talk. This period is experienced as a cataclysmic shift and is often quite terrifying. There is a feeling of being in limbo. This new clarity creates a double bind. The old way no longer works, but the new way is a complete unknown. It feels like a lose-lose. The client will sometimes be angry with the therapist during this period.

The client, almost without exception, will try to retreat to the old way. There is, however, new insight related to the old schema; therefore, the return to the old way is rejected because it no longer provides the comfort it did in the past. Insight destroyed the ability to see things through the old lens of unconsciousness. Self-awareness is a powerful thing, but it can also be, initially, painful. They feel entirely lost in this new adaptive position because it is a complete unknown. They have no idea how to behave from a position of high self-value. They never asked themselves what they wanted. So they have no idea what they want.

As the client progresses with treatment, the change in relationship dynamics may create tension and conflict as the client attempts to, for example, be assertive and establish appropriate boundaries when in the past, they were passive. Shapiro states that with couples, it is possible that such situations can be simply resolved by occasional couple sessions for psychoeducation and debriefing (Shapiro, 2018, 320). Other times, the result might lead to divorce.

Jung further explores the idea of chaos and the dark side of change. He discovered a need to embrace what is alien, dark, and chaotic in the world and the self. Jung discovered that chaos was an essential stage in alchemical work, a work that he found to be analogous to psychological work.

Jung speaks of his own descent into chaos and change:

Everything inside me is in disarray. Matters are becoming serious, and chaos is approaching. Is this the ultimate bottom? Is chaos also a foundation? If only there weren't these terrible waves. Everything breaks asunder like black billows (Jung, 2012, 298).

In our earlier discussion of the period of chaos and confusion, Jungians describe this as a period of "creative introversion," another one of those tension-of-opposites situations where something wonderful is happening below the surface in the midst of this feeling of desolation. Like the old saying, out of darkness comes light.

"Only by turning away from other men and things, did I become wholly identified with my thoughts and then found I needed to further detach" (Jung, 2012, 236a).

Jung here implies that the answer is not in the outer world, but he must turn inward for healing and wholeness within himself. The hero must answer their call. The process of EMDR therapy is self-healing. The answer is not outside but within.

The highest, most decisive experience is to be alone with one's own self. You must be alone to find out what supports you, when you find that you cannot support yourself. Only this experience can give you an indestructible foundation.[1]

EMDR, by its very nature, allows for this alone experience in which the first part is a shaking of their foundation. Often a shaking of everything they thought to be true is discovered to be a lie. Only then can the indestructible foundation of their truth and authenticity become a reality.

It is assumed that trauma processing is the most challenging work in the therapeutic process. Still, those who continue through the transformational stages often feel this stage of chaos and confusion is the worst part of the journey.

If your client feels like they are in the middle of nowhere, they are in the right place. Rejoice because something extraordinary is going to happen, although it does not feel like it. In this desert, one only needs to find a single rock to begin to build the new life, "for on this rock, I will build my church." The rock of ages, as the old gospel song says. One of the earliest forms of ritual is to place a stone on an altar (Meade, 2016, 148).

After my thirty-one-year-old son died in an accident unexpectedly, I was thrust into chaos. The response of love and support was overwhelming. People sent food, a house full of flowers, donations to my son's favorite charities, and on and on. Two of my friends and colleagues who know me, people who see the world as I do, where ritual and deep meaning are treasured, each gave me rocks. I received a total of four—the quaternity—Jung's number for wholeness. When you are hanging on by a thread, these synchronistic symbols are strengthening. Each was given to me with a story, great and sincere stories. Stories I will never forget.

All these stones except one are next to my son's urn, which we keep in a cabinet in our house. Ryan from chapter one had his family do something my son John enjoyed while they each carried their stone with them. They never even met my son, but I talked about him and the things he enjoyed. So Ryan, who is familiar with creating meaningful rituals, created a few in honor of my son. When my son was young, he was a skateboard fanatic. Ryan said his son likes to skateboard as well. Ryan gave his son the rock he was going to give me. His son kept it in his pocket and went skateboarding in honor of my son, John. Ryan took his rock out surfing. My son was not a surfer but wished he was.

My colleague Jackie Flynn gave me an ebony heart-shaped stone that I keep in my pocket. It was for me, not my deceased son, to remind me of the important work I do and that I am still alive to do it. When held up to the light, this black stone glitters within—out of the darkness, light. What we all do as therapists is we bring people out of their darkness into the light. So remember, from a few small stones placed on an altar of sorts, my family and I are building our hero's *new ordinary time*, no easy task with one member gone.

My identity has shifted. My life has been a father with two

sons. Now, I am the father of an only child. When people ask me, "Do you have any kids?" I'm not sure what to say. Yes, I have a son, and he's an engineer living in Tampa. Do I say I have two sons, but one died? Something so simple that was so easy to answer in July is now confusing for me.

Change is coming for you. Best not to fight it. When EMDR works, the best it does is it brings the person to accept their reality. In this adaptive acceptance of the truth, a new life comes.

Below is a brief description that one of my clients wrote about his experience in stage four. He is a writer and allowed me to share it.

It was hard and painful work to dismantle the self-defeating beliefs and actions that were no longer working for me. I had come to Dr. Dobo in sheer desperation, and I was grateful for what I learned through my EMDR work but I was not counting on losing my identity when I dismantled my old self.

To say this was a confusing time is an understatement. I was more than confused. I felt a void inside and a horrible sense of detachment from everything that had ever meant anything to me. This was progress? This sense of being in neutral was the most confusing feeling I had ever experienced. I missed my old self; even though my suffering had brought me to therapy, there was at least some familiarity, traditions and routines in my previous identity. Now everything was wide open, a blank slate, and I was not ready for the ambiguity. Was I becoming an unrecognizable someone to my family and friends and, even more importantly, to myself?

About the time I had entered this dark tunnel of confusion, I came upon an armadillo that was lying in the middle of the road. He was roadkill, and the buzzard intermittently picked at his innards between the scurrying of cars. The fate of the poor animal became a fitting metaphor for the death my old self was experiencing. Darwinian evolutionary thinking would argue that the armadillo had spent millennia developing its armored body to protect him against predators, but on this day, it was woefully inadequate to shield him from the overwhelming force of a speeding car. I had spent my lifetime carefully creating an identity that would deter worry, unhappiness and failure, but it had not. As my old self became exposed as the charlatan it had been, the spiritual buzzards picked every bit of it clean and had transformed me into an empty carcass.

Dr. Dobo had warned me when I started EMDR that change was inevitable and that I would lose my old view of the world, but I was not expecting this. With this much internal confusion, I doubted that I could recover from this seemingly horrible loss.

To review our integrative mindset so far:

- Avoidance causes an adversarial relationship between the person and their unconscious mind/psyche.
- Unconscious creates extreme distress, ending avoidance, causing a movement to surrender.
- Surrender is the environment in which the old self/maladaptive schema can be dismantled via self-healing.
- Dismantling causes loss of identity and a period of chaos and confusion, leaving the client in a type of limbo.

The client cannot go back to the old way for this reason—new insights cannot be undone. An additional problem is that they do not know how to behave from the new adaptive perspective. For example, if their negative cognition was *I don't matter* and suddenly shifts to *I do matter,* the client has no idea how to behave as a person that matters. This conundrum creates a period of confusion until the client figures out the new way. EMDR is a powerful therapy to accelerate this stage, stage four of the process, by usually targeting present struggles, as we will see later in book.

CHAPTER 11
THE REBIRTH AND ASSIMILATION
TRANSFORMATIONAL EMDR STAGES FIVE AND SIX

The integrative perspective helps to understand which prong of the Adaptive Information Processing Model's three-pronged approach (past, present, and future prongs) is most relevant in each stage. When a client walks in the door, we literally "take a history" to gather information. The work begins by focusing on the past. EMDR targets often begin with past events. This past as a place to start is not a hard-and-fast rule.

Let's examine what prong of the AIP model might be the focus of each of our stages, keeping in mind our simple problematic phrase of the "PAST becomes PRESENT" so targets can generalize to any time in a client's life in processing.

The early stages of avoidance, surrender, and dismantling of the old self usually address historic issues, so the work within these stages is focused on the past prong. As changes start to happen within the client, troubles occur in the present because of the client's changing perspective in themselves, in others, and in their world. The later stages—of change, loss of identity, chaos and confusion, the rebirth and assimilation of the new self—focus on the present and future prongs.

The material that EMDR targets is from these two prongs. These internal changes within the client cause behavior changes out in the world, and where there is change, there is trouble. As the new adaptive perspective becomes accepted, new boundaries are set, and assertiveness has to be imposed, which causes tension in the present and future. These new behaviors feel very uncomfortable for the clients. Assertiveness is often a struggle, so targeting present and future challenges to strengthen the new healthy but uncomfortable behavior is done.

This effort is beneficial because it dramatically and quickly strengthens the client as they begin to initiate the new uncomfortable assertive behaviors. Just saying "no" to someone can be the source of sleepless nights for the new *I do matter* client. We use EMDR to reduce anxiety about a conversation that is going to happen in the future where the client says "no" and does not back down.

Self-reinforcing component of change: The new behavior of assertiveness often feels terrible to the transforming client. Simply saying "no" to a ridiculous request by someone who frequently takes advantage of our client causes discomfort and guilt. They have the old *I don't matter* voice in their head that says, "Oh, he hates me now" or "She'll never speak to me again because I didn't do what she wanted me to do."

Subtly dramatic change starts in this stage of the process: Saying "no" is not usually a dramatic life-changing event for most, but to an *I don't matter* client, it is a moment of profound change. People send back a cold hamburger if they are dining out, but an *I don't matter* person never sends back cold food. They just eat it and think, they're probably busy in the kitchen; I don't want to bother them. After transformational EMDR, these clients send back the cold hamburger, as they should. The changes therefore seem subtle but are in fact dramatic for the client.

When these clients experience their newfound empowerment, there are usually two areas of EMDR focus. Both areas are happening in the client's PRESENT life. The focus is the present prong from Shapiro's adaptive information processing model. First, there is sometimes a fear of standing up for oneself and a reluctance to saying the assertive, boundary-setting statement. Second, once the client says the assertive statement and sets the boundary, they are often riddled with guilt and discomfort. There is a danger that they will back down in a day or two. EMDR helps to prevent this regression back to the *I don't matter* position by eliminating the inappropriate guilt. A future target that anticipates saying "no," as an example, can strengthen the client, empowering them to say what needs to be said. Notice these targets are not traumatic, just distressing.

The Phase Three Assessments might look something like this, for PRESENT and FUTURE targeting. For those of you who are not therapists, let me explain what these examples below mean within an EMDR session. Before every EMDR session, the EMDR therapist completes the procedural steps also known as Phase Three in the EMDR model. This part of the process consists of the target, the negative cognition, the positive cognition, the VOC, the emotions, SUDS and body sensations. An explanation of each is below for the non-EMDR therapists reading this.

We start with a *target,* which is the most upsetting moment of the event. This is followed by establishing the negative cognition (NC). The negative cognition should be related to the event and is generally a strong negative thought the client has about themselves when they think of the target. Negative cognitions are almost always short *I* statements, as you can see below. Then the therapist establishes a positive cognition with the client. This is an *I* statement that asks the client what they would like to think about themselves when they think of the target. It is often but not always the opposite of the negative cognition.

The VOC stands for the Validity of the Cognition, rated on a scale from one to seven. Here we ask the client, when you say to yourself the positive cognition (for example, I didn't do anything wrong), how true does that feel to you when you think about saying no to your friend? It is usually low, like a one or two. The next step is to ask the client what emotions they feel when they think of that *target* and the *negative cognition* together, and the therapist helps the client identify the *emotions* related to the *target*.

The *SUDS* scale stands for Subjective Units of Distress. This scale is a zero to ten scale where ten is the most distress and zero is no distress at all. The therapist asks how distressing does the *target* memory feel right at this moment when you think of it along with the *negative cognition* and the *emotions*. Finally, the *body* scan is the final inquiry. The therapist asks the client if they feel any body sensations when they think about the *target, negative cognitions,* and feel those *emotions*. The client may or may not have body sensations. If they do, the body sensations are documented, and if they do not, that is fine. After this is finished, we are ready to begin the bilateral stimulation. To begin the stimulation process, the client is asked to hold the *target* with the *negative cognitions* in their mind for a few seconds and then free-associate. This is the standard way we prepare to administer EMDR therapy.

Future protocol *(preparing for the assertive confrontation)*
Target: Saying no to my friend when she asks for money

NC: I'm a bad person
PC: I didn't do anything wrong
VOC: 2
Emotion: guilt, anxious, fearful
SUDS: 8
Body: shoulders tight, heart racing

Present protocol (*easing the distress after the fact*)
Target: Look of shock and anger on her face
NC: I did something wrong
PC: I didn't do anything wrong
VOC: 2
Emotion: guilt
SUDS: 8
Body: shoulders tight

This person's transformational cognition is *I don't matter*, but as you can see, other NCs are employed to maintain ego strength and the adaptive transformational cognition. These are typical situations that must be addressed as the client begins to solidify the *I matter* perspective.

You can see why these different negative cognitions become relevant as you work to strengthen all aspects of the adaptive change. Despite shifting from the maladaptive to the adaptive in session, the changes in the world are more challenging, which is why EMDR's ego-strengthening power is so valuable during these new present prong challenges.

In the rebirth stage, the therapist must actively provide assertive skills training and ego strengthening with EMDR, targeting the new healthy behaviors as the rebirth begins to assimilate. This work takes time, but if the client remains strong and moves forward in a new way, everything will improve dramatically and profoundly. They will see the world from their true and authentic self.

Let's return to Prince Harry to see a present issue and a future-pronged target. He reported that he was afraid to return to England for his grandfather's funeral. He has already shifted from *I don't matter* to *I do matter*. The adaptive shift doesn't make things easier; it just makes the struggle true, a move toward his authentic self. The struggle is in the service of his true self, not what someone else thinks he should be, so it is much easier to walk through this fire if one knows it will lead to paradise. If one knows this is in the service of my true self, my true purpose, and my authentic life, the struggle is embraced.

If I was Harry's therapist, and he stated he was afraid to return to England for his grandfather's funeral, I would have set a future template about seeing his family for the funeral. These future situations are typical for clients who have made the adaptive shift in their life. When clients change, the people around them do not like them. Future templates happen a lot around the holidays, weddings, funerals, and anytime the clients have to be around people where new boundaries are set. A hypothetical protocol for Prince Harry or any client in a similar situation might be as follows:

Hypothetical Future Template
Target: Seeing the queen for the first time at funeral
NC: I can't handle it
PC: I can handle it
VOC: 3
Emotions: anxious, afraid, angry
SUDS: 8
Body: chest is tight

The negative cognition could also be *I did something wrong*. If there is doubt about the healthy decisions the client made (saying no or setting new boundaries or whatever change the client has installed), which is common, it might be *I can't trust my judgment*. This inappropriate guilt is often experienced by the client with the transformational cognition of *I don't matter* because they are not sure they are doing the right thing. It does not feel healthy to them. It feels selfish, hence the negative cognition *I'm doing something wrong*, or *I did something wrong*. EMDR fixes this inappropriate level of responsibility and guilt.

ASSIMILATION OF THE NEW SELF

If we return to our story of the Fisher King, Parsifal need only ask the question for the king to be healed. He does not have to answer the question but simply ask it. The question Parsifal finally asks that saves the kingdom is, "Who does the Grail serve?" We can see the relevance of our story and the value of the mythological view of our work. This is the same question our clients must ask as their journey comes close to completion.

Our clients must ask, "Who does your true self serve? Is it your parents, your boss, or your spouse? The answer is, you, you first serve your true self, as you create the new life.

With a great deal of hard work, the client begins to accept and understand the new adaptive life; the struggle to accept the new authentic self is gone, and they are comfortable and empowered. The chaos and confusion stage has subsided, and the client gets familiar with the new perspective. Stage five is when the adaptive shift is understood and new behaviors that reflect the new perspective begin to take hold. Shapiro tells us that for the client to be healed, there must be an acceptance of the new adaptive schema that breaks the double bind we discussed earlier. The "damned if you do and damned if you don't" situation to "the client is free" reality.

Assimilation, which is stage six, is when the new behaviors have been engaged. Healthy boundaries are maintained, and the new life is wholly accepted. Once the new assertive behaviors are engaged, they become self-reinforcing. The client understands how to set limits. They set them. People around them know that the client has these limits, so they do not push against them. A new homeostasis sets in, and the new healthy perspective for our hero's ordinary time begins.

As we predicted and even warned the client, the way they view themselves and others has changed. The way they engage the world and the way they allow the world to engage them has changed. The person shifts to a more authentic self, a self with newfound value and purpose.

CHAPTER 12

THE JUNGIAN LEXICON
ENHANCING GENERALIZATION

J ung's description of unconscious material helps the clinician identify rarely noticed statements. Most clinicians notice body sensations but never see them as communication from the unconscious. When the therapist becomes aware of this new language, generalizability increases, meaning the client moves out of distressful memories quicker and more efficiently. This language is exponentially more potent than the typical thoughts, feelings, images, memories, and body sensations that clinicians are trained to identify. It is no wonder that clinicians do not learn to discern powerful phrases from unimportant phrases because Francine Shapiro instructs the trainee to never differentiate or emphases a part of the response to the query. She is wrong. This is the one or two times that I disagree with her. The results are clear, discernment and differentiation of the material that is provided by the clients is essential. It separates a good EMDR therapist from an extraordinary EMDR therapist.

As we proceed, the therapist will learn to differentiate high-value material in the client responses from neutral, moderate or low-value material. Without exception, the Jungian lexicon is of highest value when it occurs in the EMDR process. This chapter will clarify what exactly this means to the therapist and how to implement this new understanding.

The Jungian material will enhance the processing throughout the neural networks Shapiro identifies. Jung implores, "We have a right on purely empirical grounds to treat the contents of the unconscious just as real as the things of the outside world."[1] The contents of the unconscious are more real, generalizable, and non-specific, as symbols do not simply move through a person's life. Symbols move through thousands of years of history, breaking the bond of time and space.

JUNG'S LEXICON OF THE UNCONSCIOUS

1. Characteristic One: Sense and nonsense are of equal value.
"The highest truth is one and the same with the absurd. Meaning requires absurdity, and absurdity requires meaning." The soul (unconscious) speaks in sense and nonsense. Supreme meaning is the "melting together of meaning and absurdities—of sense and nonsense." (Jung, 2012, 242a). The EMDR therapist should not disregard nonsense. The EMDR therapist has no problem attending to material that makes sense, but the same value, perhaps even more attention, should be given to *nonsense*. An example of nonsense was when a client reported during an EMDR session that she saw an image of an ornate wooden box. She said, "There is nothing in the box, but it's not empty." This box was profoundly healing for her as the session proceeded. We will discuss this case a little later.

2. The psyche speaks in common hackneyed language (Jung, 2012, 23).

Categories below:

Clichés: It came out of the blue. No use crying over spilled milk. I was dancing to their tune, not mine. I'm always walking on thin ice.

Metaphors: I was running around like a chicken without a head. It hit me like a freight train.

Colloquialism: Red up your room. That dog won't hunt. He's a bubble off center.

Hackneyed phrases: Last but not least. We can walk and chew gum at the same time. Two sides of the same coin. At the end of the day. You see what I mean.

Common Phrases: I got to let go. I don't know what to do. I can't get out. No one ever helped me. 'Cause I said so.

This material is unremarkable and therefore easy to overlook. Below is a list that identifies dozens of these unremarkable phrases that were spoken during the various phases of EMDR. The reason they are so powerful is because they are highly generalizable to hundreds of moments in the client's life. Each generalized phrase can be understood as a different way to express the negative cognition. Just look at the last phrase in our common phrases group, "because I said so." How many times do you think my client heard this phrase? Thousands of times. This phrase implies that his voice did not matter; only his mother's voice did. If you go with this phrase, it will generalize to the multitude of times he heard this phrase.

GENERALIZABLE MATERIAL: THE PHRASE, JUNGIAN CATEGORY AND EMDR PHASES

Phrase (Jung's Description/**Phase of Occurrence**)

- I got to get out of here. (Common phrase/**Phase Four**)
- My best is never good enough. (Common phrase/**Phase One**)
- It came out of the blue. (Cliché/**Phase Four**)
- A can of flat Dr. Pepper (Image, nonsense/**Phase Four**)
- What am I going to do? (Common phrase/**Phase Four**)
- I don't want her taking my french fry. (Nonsense/**Phase Eight & follow up**)
- The box didn't have anything in it, but it wasn't empty. (Nonsense/**Phase Four**)

- I'm seeing a field of pink petunias. (Image/**Phase Five**)
- I was like a chicken without a head. (Metaphor/**Phase Four**)
- I'm a dancing turtle. (Image/**Phase Five**)
- I'm in a glass jar seen but not heard. (Image/**Phase Four**)
- I'm ready to get my hands dirty. (Common Phrase/**Phase One**)
- I had to get out of there. (Common Phrase/**Phase Eight & follow up**)
- I'm stuck in soft candy. (Image/**Phase Four**)

SYMBOLS AND IMAGES ARE THE HIGHEST-VALUE RESPONSES

Neither reason nor feeling can produce symbols, which must arise unconsciously and spontaneously through the vehicle of the imagination, which "alone has the power to supply the will with a content of such a nature that it can unite the opposites" (Jung, 1969, vol. 6, § 179). Uniting the opposite is one of the goals of Jungian therapy. (Can be thought of as an integration of emotional distress or Shapiro's shift from maladaptive to the adaptive.) Jung implies respect for both internal and external processes, as does EMDR. EMDR is done in silence (internal process), but as we know in transformational stages four and five, external changes occur in the client's life that must be managed and assimilated.

Both models cause significant internal change, causing our "subtly dramatic" external changes for the person as we assist them in finding their healthy, adaptive and authentic self.

It is crucial as you integrate Jung with EMDR that you listen for phrases described by Jung. If you are unsure whether or not a phrase is a Jungian one or not, ask yourself if the client's negative cognition is represented in that phrase. Do you think this phrase is generalizable to other times in the client's life? If the answer is yes, you have started integrating Jung with Shapiro's EMDR therapy. Examples of phrases that match the client's negative cognition are below:

Negative cognition manifested in Jungian phrase and phase in which it occurred

Client's NC—Jungian Valued Material — Phase
I don't matter — I never got a break. — **Phase Three**

I'm in danger — I got to get out of here. — **Phase Four**

I'm in danger — There's nowhere to go. — **Dream**

I don't matter — I better not push it. — **Phase Four**

I can't handle it — I can't get out. — **Phase Four**

I'm not in control — It came out of the blue. — **Phase Four**

I don't matter — Flat Dr. Pepper — **Phase Four**

I'm not good enough — I'm a dancing turtle. — **Phase Five**

I don't matter — I danced to their tune, not mine. — **Phase Five**

These phrases manifested during EMDR processing and were linked to dozens of moments in the client's life. These phrases enhance generalizability.

Each phrase represents the core negative cognition in some way. Let's examine the generalizability of the first phrase in the chart of generalizable material.

"I GOT TO GET OUT OF HERE."

This phrase occurred with a client who had a fear of elevators. When she was in a situation where riding an elevator could not be avoided, she had but one thought: I got to get out of here! I got to get out of here! During EMDR processing, she stated this phrase, and we went with it. It linked to dozens of memories. Here are a few:

1. She was in a terrible (but nonviolent) marriage. She had to get out of the marriage, an "I got to get out of here" connected to her desolate life.

2. She was previously in a violently abusive relationship. Her husband was on top of her, banging her head on the bathroom floor. She remembers thinking, "I got to get out of here. I'm going to die here." (There were

many situations like this one that occurred in this relationship.) "I got to get out of here" is a high-value phrase to process this violence. It is high-value because of the potential for generalization. The skill to discern the difference increases the efficiency of the therapist and reduces the distress the client will endure during the session.

3. She was moving her horse into a trailer, and it acted up. She was trapped in the trailer while this was happening. "I got to get out of here or I'm going to die in here."

4. There were many other less traumatic events as well. One was being afraid to ask her first-grade teacher to use the bathroom. "I got to get out of here, or I'm going to wet myself."

By identifying this unremarkable phrase and going with it, connections are made. The process immediately started to generalize. It is no wonder she feared the elevator; this phrase linked to some of the most terrifying and embarrassing moments in her life.

In the following transcript, see if you can recognize:

1. Implicit memory fragments being revealed and put in context.

2. Self-healing and client's adamant statement that he did this on his own. If the therapist intervenes, they deprive the client of the joy of figuring the problem out for themselves. Don't do that! Keep your cleverness to yourself.

3. Evidence of generalizability.

4. Revealing hidden shadow material that has been hidden for over fifty years.
5. Profound psychological change.
6. Jungian lexicon and what to go with. Identify the high-value phrase. What would you isolate and go with?

What are you noticing?

Well, the guilt about going to Vietnam was there. I had never known that. I inconvenienced my family by getting drafted. Okay, I flunked out of college. I got suspended for a semester, fucked up, got drafted and how they see me. I kept on screwing up. That's part of the continuum, and that hasn't stopped, in their opinion. Even with the thing about the house in Maine, I can't go near it with my pets. I'm allowed in there but not my pets. They just see me as a lesser class of being and lesser class of being. Even my belief system, because he's this psychologist—top-down shit. I have no validity whatsoever. It comes back to this whole thing ... what the fuck ... You know, I was lucky I didn't kill myself in Vietnam.

In this above paragraph I isolated the unusual phrase and ignored the rest of the response to the query. Can you identify the phrase I isolated and went with?

What are you noticing?

I am so much better than he has been seeing me, than my family's been seeing me. I am so much better. I saw him doing it to other people, not just me. That's just what he does to keep himself up. My father did it, and my brother really did it. It wasn't really about Vietnam. It was just about that whole thing. Like, here's a feather I have in my cap, and he tries to knock it out. You don't get to do that. Fuck you. Don't ever say that again. You don't dare. You don't have the right. Don't. Stop. It's like the lady on the tennis court. Stop. I am better. I expanded and surrounded his little shithole of a life.

In this above paragraph, I isolated the unusual phrase and ignored the rest of the response to the query. Can you identify the phrase I isolated and went with?

Therapist: Okay, let's go with that ...
Client: Okay, but I got there on my own.
Therapist: I know. You always get there on your own. I don't worry.

What are you noticing?
That just went through everything. People, my brother, ex-wives, business partners. That was the old me. I played to their tune, not mine.

In this above paragraph, I isolated the unusual phrase and ignored the rest of the response to the query. Can you identify the phrase I isolated and went with?

What are you noticing?
I'm free. They're behind and below me. The energy is I'm just expanding, filled with grace and white light. They are fading. They are behind me and below me, fading away.

By utilizing high-value material, the shift from maladaptive perspective to adaptive perspective happens in minutes.

Accelerated process: All of the above integrative material happened in this fourteen-minute EMDR processing session, including Phase Three. The client came in highly agitated and angry, and in minutes he was calm and stated, "I'm free."

Answer to question one: Implicit memory fragments being revealed and put in context.
"I saw him doing it to other people, not just me. That's just what he does to keep himself up."

Answer to question 2: Evidence that client wanted to self-heal:
Client: Okay, but I got there on my own.
Therapist: I know. You always get there on your own. I don't worry.

Response to question 3: Evidence of generalizability in his response: "That just went through everything. People, my brother, ex-wives, business partners. That was the old me."

Response to question 4: Evidence of shadow material, hidden but then revealed.
"Well, the guilt about going to Vietnam was there. I had never known that."

Response to question 5: Profound psychological change.
"I'm free. They're behind and below me. The energy is I'm just expanding, filled with grace and white light."

Responses to Question 6: Jungian lexicon.
This was isolated as the most high-value material in the response. The other material was ignored.

- **Response one:** "They see me as a lesser class of being."
- **Response two**: "Here's a feather I have in my cap, and he tried to knock it out too."
- **Response three**: "I played to their tune, not mine."

If you wonder why these statements are of higher value than anything else the client says, simply ask yourself: How often did his father and brother make him feel like a lesser class of being in his life? Hundreds of times, practically every day of his life growing up. Therefore, this statement is the most powerful and has the highest value. He stated the same with the other clichés in the other query responses. Of course, we do not always get so many clichés, but I know this client, and he often will eventually sum up his response with a cliché, so I wait, watch and listen for it.

THE UNCONSCIOUS SPEAKS THROUGH THE BODY

For an EMDR therapist, there is a great deal of emphasis on working with the body. What is rarely understood is the metaphor the body brings to the process through the unconscious. If we know that the unconscious speaks in metaphors and clichés, the unconscious creates metaphors through the body. Well, it does. Below are some common interweaves when a body sensation occurs. These are also ways to understand the language of the body as it speaks to us through the body.

EMDR therapists usually have three choices when a body sensation occurs during a session.

1. They can do a somatic float back by simply bringing the attention to the body, then we ask the client to

close their eyes and to float back to an earlier time they felt that body sensation. This often results in a profound connection to their past.

2. We can continue as normal and say, "Go with that."
3. They can use one of the metaphoric interweaves for the body that are listed below.

Somatic Interweaves

- If the client's back hurts: "Who has betrayed you, stabbed you in the back?" Also, a backache with no medical issue is usually a person who *does not matter*. They cannot stand up for themselves. "They need to get a spine."
- Client's neck hurts: "Who is a pain in your neck right now?"
- Client has stomach problems: "Who kicked you in the gut, knocked the wind out of you?"
- Client's chest hurts: "Who has broken your heart?"
- Client's throat gets tight during processing: "When did you not have a voice?"
- Client reports itchy skin or hives: "Who gets under your skin?"
- Client feels like choking: "Is there a situation in your life that is hard to swallow?"
- The client's mouth is dry: Often *I don't matter* people who did not have a voice have a dry mouth. Also, you might ask, "Has anything happened to you that leaves a bad taste in your mouth?"

SYNCHRONICITY: THE UNIVERSE IS HELPING; TRY TO LISTEN

Synchronicity is defined as a meaningful coincidence. It can be a moment when your inner life collides with the external world. If you attend to your dreams, this happens quite often. A colleague of mine and I were discussing dreams. She dreamed of being in a house where two attackers were invading her home. She started to fight them off. A few months later, as she brushed her teeth, a new insight came out of nowhere about the dream. Her inner voice said to her, "Those attackers are you." Wow. When an unexpected interior dream experience collides with the outer world to provide new insight about oneself, this collision is an example of a synchronistic event. Sometimes they happen during therapy. For me, they often happen to trainees who come to my EMDR basic training. Here are two examples:

I was demonstrating EMDR in training with Jackie Flynn, LMHC. We targeted a scary event that happened to her. While she was out of town, her daughter was in a car accident. She called her boyfriend to check on her daughter, who was at home after the accident. During our EMDR processing in training, the very moment she was thinking about her boyfriend being at home to take care of things, my Ring app went off on my phone in the training. She said, "I was just thinking of him getting there, and the Ring app went off on my phone in my mind as he approached the front door at that exact moment yours just did, which was reassuring because I knew he was there, and everything would be all right."

The second event was at a training. One of the trainees was biracial. She does not trust white girls, especially white, blond girls, because they have betrayed her throughout her life. I did not know about her discomfort and distrust of white girls. Her practice partner was white, fair, with freckles, from Alabama. My bira-cial trainee did not say anything and was okay working with her partner. She had attended a mini EMDR training and brought her own EMDR machine to the training. When we started practicing, the left side of the machine stopped working. I changed the batteries and messed with it to see if I could get it to work, but I couldn't. This trainee was unhappy because she preferred not to get close to this white woman, and she certainly did not want to touch her, but she had no choice because her machine was broken.

As it turned out, the two of them had a great experience. Both felt safe with each other and did great work together. The message was, "I can trust some white girls." The funny thing was on the last day of the training, when we were finished practicing, the machine worked just fine. There was no problem with the device. The machine malfunctioned only long enough for the clients to get close to one another.

There was a client whose dog was acting up before he left for our session together. The plan was to target his abusive mother. When he walked in for our session, immediately, he began to rant about his wife's dog (a dog he is incredibly fond of). This client is always cool, calm, and collected. His affect was agitated when he walked in for his session, which I had never seen before in his presentation. He described his morning.

"My wife's stupid dog would not stop barking today. It was barking and barking. No matter what I did, it wouldn't stop barking. It was out of control. There was no reason for it to be barking, nothing going on outside, but he would not stop. It was like he was possessed. He never does that. I never saw him act like that before. I was furious. I just had to get out of there. I told my wife, 'I got to get out of here. I'm going to the diner to get a coffee before I go to see Dobo,' and I left."

We were preparing to target his abusive mother, but I followed the client, and it seems like this barking dog is a better choice. This is one of those moments where nonsense wins out over sense. This barking dog led to the most profound EMDR session we ever had together. My client had been in many situations where he could have died, and the refrain for each of these situations was, "I got to get out of here." This phrase is what he said to himself during each of these traumatic events. If you notice from the text above, he said, and I quote, "I told my wife, *'I got to get out of here.* I'm going to the diner to get a coffee before I go to see Dobo,' and I left."

So is this a coincidence, or a meaningful coincidence, our synchronistic event? Is it the universe conspiring to help me help my clients? This single statement connected to hidden memories he never shared. He remembered being trapped in a shipwreck while scuba diving and thought he was going to drown. He remembered saying to himself over and over again, "I got to get out of here" while trapped. He remembered being held up at gunpoint while working in a pawn shop, thinking to himself, "I got to get out of here." There is a force greater than our frontal lobe helping us help our clients. I hope you will be open to such events. Once you are open to these things, they happen frequently. And the idea that the unconscious is an ally becomes a very real and powerful thing to attend to in your work.

PART THREE

TOOLS
FOR DEVELOPING
YOUR
INNER GENIUS

THE ROAD
TO EXCELLENCE

CHAPTER 13

FINDING YOUR PLACE OF POWER
THE THERAPIST'S CALL TO ADVENTURE

First, let me say that most therapists will not do what this section suggests. The following activities will be challenging because social media and constant access to devices destroy our ability to think deeply about anything. This statement is not hyperbole; it is a scientific fact. This is why creators of social media platforms do not let their children anywhere near a social platform.

A study commissioned by Hewlett-Packard looked at the IQ of some of their workers: one group, when they were not permitted to be interrupted, and the other group, which was interrupted on a typical day addressing emails and phone calls. They found that the interrupted group lost ten IQ points.

These interruptions might not seem like much. But a similar test was done where a group of subjects smoked cannabis vs. a non-cannabis-smoking group. The cannabis group only lost five IQ points, so interruptions are twice as impactful on IQ as cannabis.

The interruption study did not even include social media

interruptions like Facebook or Instagram, just calls and emails. The research showed these interruptions had a devastating effect on deep thinking (Hari, 2021, 39).

A small research study among college students demonstrated the effect of social media on our ability to tolerate being bored. They discovered that the average college student could handle being bored for only nineteen seconds before looking for stimulation on their devices. These activities in this part of the book require building new concentration muscles. You will need to focus for half an hour and sometimes longer. The devices have to be locked up initially and out of reach when you engage in the activities recommended in the final part of this book.

You may have an internal fight on your hands and give up on these processes because they are too dull. The need for stimulation is a real threat. You do not get any "likes" or "shares" by writing something in your journal. The only person you are getting to know is you. This exploration inward is deadly serious business. I hope you have the courage and conviction to continue this internal work. Once you start to contact your inner self, the true mystery of the psyche and perhaps your life itself will be revealed to you. Remember what Charles Bukowski said:

> *there is no other feeling like it.*
> *you will be alone with the gods*
> *and the nights will flame with*
> *fire. ...*
>
> *you will ride death straight to*
> *hell,*
> *your perfect laughter,*
> *the only good fight*
> *now.* [1]

Accessing the inner genius can only occur when you can be still and listen to your inner self. Meditation is a good practice for developing this skill, but just regular introspection about your life is an excellent way to be more connected to your inner self. Dreams are a superb doorway into your inner reality, which you will learn to explore in the final chapter of this book. The subsequent chapters discuss ways to move inward to get to your authentic self, which requires psychological health and self-awareness.

Most people are not deliberate when they begin to journal. They get a notebook, grab a pen, and start journaling something, or they may scribble a dream they recall. It is a haphazard way to start and will rarely be maintained. The following pages will ask that you put away all devices and distractions and begin this mindful process of creating your ritual space. The first step is finding your place of power, much like Carlos Castaneda did in the first chapter.

THE QUEST FOR YOUR PLACE OF POWER

First, it is necessary to give the search for your place of power meaning with a ritual. Below are suggestions, not rules to follow rigidly. This first step requires your intuition to aid in creating a ritual compatible with your life experience, your belief system, and your personality.

If we are planning to encounter your inner reality, your soul, your collective unconscious, whatever you want to call it, it is necessary to discover a place where you feel comfortable, at peace, and safe. Let's examine some ways to get started.

LOGISTIC PREPARATIONS FOR THE SEARCH

You should pick a day and a time in advance. This planning will give you time to make any necessary preparation that you need to do on the day of the search. Setting a date provides meaning and commitment. You might choose a date with some special significance, perhaps a birthday or an anniversary, a day in memory of the death of a loved one in whose honor you are beginning this change. It could be a day that marks the beginning of a new part of your life. If you cannot think of such a date, choose any date, at least a few days in advance, to make the necessary preparations for this first step of your inner journey.

You might share the decision with others to enlist emotional support. Tell your friends and family that you plan to begin this journaling process. Communicating your intentions will help prepare those close to you for the changes due to this work. We know when combined with EMDR, the changes can be significant. For example, if you live with others, they will know that your quiet time is essential. We hope they will be supportive and honor your need for a daily period of solitude. Please be selfish about this time, because you are entitled to it. It is a small investment in self-care.

You may, however, choose to keep the decision private, telling no one. Some people derive power from keeping this work to themselves. This internal effort is sacred work, so if you feel more comfortable keeping it a secret, then do so. Again, the choice is yours.

Once you decide on a date, begin preparing. If you have children, you may want to get a babysitter for the day of the search. If your significant other is going to be at home, you may wish to discuss this process with them so that you will not be disturbed.

You must turn off cellphones, iPad, computers, televisions, or anything else that might disrupt this first step.

Ritual preparation can range from minimal to extravagant. The goal is to make the process meaningful and sacred to you. A range of suggestions is described below. These suggestions are not comprehensive but do provide a range and variety of possibilities. You can use these or create your own.

Some clients fast the day before and the day of the search. I do not fast, but people have shared with me the benefits they feel from fasting during this process. Fasting is a powerful way to create a sacred and holy context in a spiritual activity. Fasting is usually something people bring to this inner work from their existing religious beliefs. Combining preexisting religious practices with the ritual container is a powerful combination for creating ritual; however, it is not necessary if you do not utilize such practices. Combining these two behaviors intensifies one's spiritual belief and causes me to experience a much stronger sense of spirituality.

Objects of significance can bring powerful meaning to an encounter with the unconscious. You can keep these objects with you during the search, which is a powerful way to get a personal sense of sacredness to your safe place.

One client told me that her mother had died when she was young, and she was given her engagement and wedding ring after her death. She had never put them on her finger until the day she chose to search for her place, thus beginning her inner journey.

Her initial inner work was coming to terms with the loss of her mother. She put her mother's rings on during the search for her space, and the simple act of putting on these rings for the first time made this process holy, sacred, and very meaningful. These ritual objects made what might have been a rather ordinary task a truly extraordinary experience—a profoundly personal and moving ritual.

She keeps these rings in a little jewelry box next to her journal in her place. These rings help her create and maintain her place's sacredness, enhancing her inner journey and worldly life. She stated, "Although my mom is no longer with me, I feel a connection to her when I am in my place of power."

Where is your place of power? In what room is it? Usually, you already have your place of power in your home. When you end the day, take your shoes off to relax, where do you sit? Do you sit in the same place? You probably do. Your place of power is there. Sometimes this is a high-traffic area, and you may need to find a different location for this internal work. Being mindful of where you feel comfortable is the key. Remember, if you try a place and find it doesn't feel right, you can change and move to a different location until you find your space.

TOOLS FOR THE JOURNEY

Now that you have discovered your place and made it sacred using your personalized ritual, the time comes to begin the inner work.

Let's begin with a brief discussion on how to choose a journal. I know people want to use their devices for their journals or to work on their dreams. In the end, the decision is yours. I know younger adults who do not know the world without an iPhone or computer are reading this. Some never learned to write cursive, so the idea of writing with a pen and paper seems very foreign. I would implore you to try to bring your dreams and thoughts out of the unconscious mind's world and into your journal's three-dimensional world, not the two-dimensional world of your devices. Creating a sense of ritual in every aspect of this work is essential.

Choosing a journal and ink pen should be a mindful process, even sacred. The journal you choose is going to contain very personal and intimate material. The essence of your relationship with your inner self will appear on the pages of your journal. This journal will be your companion for a substantial period, so feel comfortable with it and treat it respectfully.

Although going to the bookstore may seem like an ordinary experience, remember we are trying to create extraordinary experiences out of the ordinary. This mindful method of establishing the ritual elements may seem silly at first. Still, scientific evidence supports the notion that creating a sense of sacredness in an activity makes it more powerful and effective. A study by Russell E. Phipps II and Kenneth Pargament proved that subjects who believed their dreams were sanctified (the term they used in their research) experienced more positive life changes. Subjects that did not have the sanctified perspective had a less profound experience.[2] Carefully choosing the journal and pen is an essential first step in creating a sacred environment for this inner work to thrive. Rituals, by definition, take an ordinary activity and make it extraordinary.

As I reflect on the array of journals I have used in the past forty years, I notice that each one represented, in a subtle way, who I was at that time in my life. For example, when I was a starving undergraduate musician, my journals were all the inexpensive wire-bound notebooks I used to take notes for college classes. I was familiar with these notebooks. I knew which style I preferred because they were an essential part of my life during that time.

In the '70s and early '80s, it was challenging to find hardcover journals. The local bookstores rarely carried any journals at all. I believe the first ones were called *The Blank Book*, but these were very small and stiff, which made them hard to write in. Later the bookstores began to carry journals that were more to my liking. The first time I saw a lined hardcover journal in a bookstore, I bought three because I had never seen them before and thought I might never see them again. Fortunately, I was wrong. Most bookstores now have an incredible selection of journals. Amazon has an endless choice of journals in all shapes and price ranges. Your inner journey awaits you there.

THE SEARCH FOR YOUR PERSONAL JOURNAL

The process of searching for a journal is similar to the process of searching for your place of power. The same techniques used to discover your place of power can be used in choosing a journal. For example, you can take a ritual object along on the journey to the bookstore.

Please do not minimize or disregard the importance of the ritual component. You saw that the day Ryan spent performing acts in honor of my son were rituals. These frequent acts that Ryan and his son do often are ordinary until they carry a stone with them during the act in honor of my deceased son; then the ordinary act becomes extraordinary—the very definition of a ritual. Make the choice of the journal and pen a holy process, like the research study—sanctified. The process can be utterly secular if you do not believe in such things. It is entirely up to you. It should not be treated like a trip to the grocery store but approached carefully and diligently. The more effort you make to turn this seemingly ordinary experience into something extraordinary, the better your results will be.

Choosing a journal has a lot to do with how it feels in your hands. Hold each one and see how easy it is for the pages to stay open while you write. You do not want a journal that you have to wrestle with just to make an entry. Looks are important, too. My journals look serious; they're usually dark-colored and solid these days.

My friend Marty had a powerful synchronistic experience with Winnie the Pooh. He had a dream of Winnie the Pooh about a deceased friend. That morning he went for a run and found a solid red playing card on the ground. For some reason, he reached for it to see what was on the other side, only to discover it had a picture of Winnie the Pooh on it. As you may have guessed, he sought out a brightly colored journal with *Winnie the Pooh* prominently displayed on the cover.

My wife loves flowers, and her choice usually has a floral cover. Take your time and choose a journal that looks and feels comfortable to you.

One should not be too frugal when picking a journal or a pen. If your finances are limited, then frugality is the order of the day, but the more expensive something is, the more value we place on it and the more likely we are to use it but also keep it safe.

As a therapist, I have worked in agencies where the state paid for my services, and as a consequence, the patients had little or no expense. They treated the service as if it had no value because it was free. These clients would miss appointments without calling to cancel, show up late, and do little work to improve their situation.

When I could charge a person an appropriate fee for my services, people would pay and treat the work as having high value. These patients rarely missed their appointment; if they did, they would call in advance. These clients listened to every word I said because they were paying a lot of money for these words, so what I had to say had a great deal of value. The quality of my work was the same in both settings, but my value was perceived very differently when people had no financial interest in the process.

This same idea applies to your journal and pen. The more you can afford to pay for a journal, the more value it will have, hence the more likely you will use it. If your pen is expensive, you will be careful not to lose it or use it carelessly, but if it's inexpensive, your risk of losing it is high. If you cannot afford this extravagance, that is okay. When I began this work, my tools were cheap, but I respected them.

Journals on average last six to eight months. Nevertheless, at times you might fill three journals in six months. At times one will last two years. You may experience an ebb and flow in your life and with the journal. Making daily journal entries is the best practice. Otherwise, you are in danger of stopping the process, thus returning to the old way of distractions, hurrying, and losing the inner relationship. A daily entry is an excellent way to ensure a continuation of the work. Even if the only comment is, "Nothing to say today," at least you went to the journal for a brief moment. If you skip one day and then another, the danger of stopping this practice altogether becomes very real.

Remember that you do not have to fill a journal before you change or get a new one. If you do not like a particular journal for some reason, stop using it and get a new one, because if you do not like the journal, you will not use it. Sometimes a fresh start is needed, and getting a new journal whenever one feels compelled is a way to re-motivate yourself.

In our life's journey, we will experience significant endings and beginnings. These events do not always coincide with the completion of a journal. If a new stage in your life is beginning and you feel that choosing a new journal would be a powerful ritual component to this new stage in your life, get a new journal to mark this new beginning. If you need to complete each page of every journal, that is fine, but it is not the only way to journal.

Changing when you need to change is always acceptable. Flexibility is an essential component of this work.

If the process feels forced or stale, then change something. Change the time of day you do the inner work, start a dream notebook, keep the journal separate from the dream work, draw or write poetry rather than writing in a narrative, or read other books on the subject.

A time away from the journal might be okay. I have taken extended breaks from this work. If you feel that a break from the journal is needed, then take a break, but the date when the work is to resume should be determined before you take this break, and you must have the discipline to resume on the predetermined date. Without such a plan, the break can easily end your dedication to the inner work.

Do not feel you must use the journal the same way every day. What you need from the journal today will be very different from what you will need from it in ten years. Inner work is not logical or linear but fluid and ever-changing. You must be flexible.

THE PEN

The same process of choosing a journal should be used in selecting an ink pen. Again, it is essential to hold the pen; it is important to make sure the pen feels comfortable. I used the same ink pen for over fifteen years, therefore, I cannot imagine going to my journal with a different pen in my hand. I have owned very few objects for as long as I owned this ink pen, so I feel a strong attachment to this object. There is a certain power that this pen has for me that no other pen has. The pen eventually failed; now, I use a pen a friend made for me. I got the wooden pen blocks from an olive tree in Jerusalem, and he created a handmade pen out of it for me.

My wife bought me a fantastic pen that has black and red ink. I use this for my dreams. I write the dream in red ink and my thoughts about the dream in black. I can, at a glance, see what entries my dreams are (red ink) and what entries are the interpretations of the dream (black ink). You have to find what works for you.

If you talk to an artist, they have a particular set of brushes that they use and would not think of changing. When I was a child, the priest in our parish spoke to our Sunday School class about his chalice. He explained that his parents bought this for him on the day he was ordained a priest, and he had used it for over thirty years. He would not think of celebrating mass with a different chalice.

My cousin is an expert drywall finisher. He had a drywall knife that was so old and used that the blade was half its original size. He hated to replace it, but he had no choice. He almost cried when he retired that blade. He must have had hundreds of miles literally on that blade finishing houses.

These ordinary objects become extraordinary when we use them in our daily rituals. We make them holy by respecting and appreciating them. We do not do this much anymore. This holding on to special items is a lost art. We are always looking for the newest model or version of things. We are a disposable society. I hope that you will become less disposable and develop more respect for the things around you.

As you journal, small things that previously went unnoticed become important. An example would be a my friend's tattered Winnie the Pooh card he found on the street or Anne's mother's wedding ring, my ink pen, or the stone gifts I received in honor of my son, John. These objects carry great importance and internal value that help us connect with our inner selves. If you can bring something like this to your place of power with your journal and pen, the more sacred the place and the work becomes.

WHEN IN DOUBT ... FAKE IT

You may initially have difficulty making this process sacred. You may say to yourself, "I do not know if I feel that my journal or pen is right for me. I do not feel holy or sacred when I use these things." This uncertainty is expected. You must be patient, trusting that these things will happen when the time is right. The early work is about sowing the seeds of sacredness and becoming comfortable with solitude and the journal.

Alcoholics Anonymous has an expression that they teach their members, "Fake it till you make it." This saying usually refers to accepting the reality of a higher power, which some members have difficulty doing. AA asks these members just to pretend until they experience it. Muhammad Ali offers the same advice. He said, "To be a great champion, you must believe you are the best. If you're not, pretend you are." If you struggle with this part of the process, I will encourage you to do the same. Fake it until you make it!

PREPARING THE JOURNAL

You should number each page of the journal. Many come numbered these days, but if not, the pages should be numbered. You can number the pages all at once, or you can number the pages as you move through the journal—a few pages at a time. Number the journal pages to track similar dreams with reoccurring symbols you encounter at night. Page numbers help to relocate a related dream or event, thus connecting dream sequences.

Write your name, address, phone number(s), and e-mail

address on your journal's front and back cover. Although my journal rarely leaves my home, I sometimes take it with me on business trips or vacations, and although it has little value to anyone else, it has great value to me. Identifying information increases the likelihood that it will be returned if lost.

I always write a statement on the front inside cover that notifies anyone who may find my journal that I will give a fifty-dollar reward to the person who finds and returns the journal to me. I have never lost a journal, but if I ever do happen to lose it, this statement dramatically increases the possibility that it will be returned.

The material in the journal is very private. The contents are not to be read by anyone without your permission.

An example of a privacy statement follows: "The contents of this journal are extremely private, and I respectfully ask that you not read the contents without my permission." I close by printing and signing my name at the end of this statement.

Journals are not like the Hollywood journals you read about with salacious details of the scandal. Soul work is usually interesting only to the person experiencing the process and their therapist if they are working with a companion on this journey. Reading through twenty-five or thirty dreams belonging to someone else is boring. The interesting aspect is in the personal process of interpreting, not reading what someone else has written.

These journal preparations have become part of my ritual. When I end a journal, I summarize the journal's contents—the most significant events—in the final pages. I also write the names of people who have experienced important events that I know, for example, the names and dates of any deaths, births, or marriages. When a journal is complete, I usually write on the spine the first and last date of the entries and put the book away.

Morton Kelsey has written extensively on this subject. His work has a strong Christian base. He prays in his journal, writes petitions to God, and keeps a list of people to pray for, both living and dead. These religious ideas can be compelling when used with a journal. Kelsey divides his journal into two sections: the front section, where he writes about his daily or outer world, and the back section, where he records his inner work with dreams and the spiritual realm. Some of my clients use two separate journals, one for dream work and the other for everything else.

I have tried many ways, but I prefer all my journal entries for a particular day to be exactly that, my journal entries for that day, and I want them to all be in the same place—the day they occurred. So my thoughts and dreams are all documented when they occurred in the same place. Do what feels comfortable to you, and do not be afraid to experiment or change your mind from time to time.

Do not use the journal for anything other than journaling. It should not be used for taking phone messages or writing grocery lists. Using the journal for these daily mundane activities cheapens its value, reduces its power and meaning, and makes it more challenging to create a sense of sacredness.

Remember, the pages of your journal document encounters with your soul; naturally, this should be treated with extreme respect.

THE BEGINNING ENTRY

My daily entry always begins with the date, day of the week and the approximate time followed by a sentence that is a reminder of the day—a memory statement. This statement describes something that was unique about the day.

Sample Entry Memory Statement:
August 18, 2021, Monday 10 p.m.
I had lunch with Tom and his wife at The Sandwich Café.

That's it; that's my memory statement. All I need is a brief statement reflecting that day's events.

The more you practice this statement, the more skillful you will become in creating these short, efficient accounts that remind you of the day. A new awareness of what you're doing each day will develop, and the memory statement will become easy to create.

This simple statement reminds me of what I was doing before lunch and what I did after lunch. I recall what we talked about, and I know that we had never been to this restaurant before, making it a unique event. Without such a statement, this day begins to blur with the next, and much is forgotten. You may need three sentences describing the morning, afternoon, and then evening, which is fine, but brevity is the goal.

Developing this skill is essential. The journal is not a laundry list of the day's events; it is not a daily planner or a diary but an exploration inward toward meaningful thoughts, feelings, motivations, dreams, and your truth. It is, however, essential to know what is going on in your daily life during a particular day.

That is why these essential memory statements are important and are an excellent place to start the daily entry.

CHAPTER 14
JOURNALING IDEAS
MOVING INWARD

The first techniques presented here are general ones designed to facilitate inner exploration and outer examination of yourself. Like the definition of ritual—changing the ordinary into the extraordinary—these techniques may seem unremarkable, but do not be fooled by their simplicity, because they are powerful when practiced with commitment and devotion.

Ask yourself, "What did I learn today?" This question is simple but very effective. In order to answer it, you must mentally review the entire day, searching for a significant learning experience. This question can address the spirit, relationships, or the world. It can be work-related, about a misunderstanding with someone or about an inner spiritual conflict that causes distress.

This question can give rise to a great deal of introspection in all areas of your life. You can stop reading right here and begin working with this one question for the rest of your life. Many journal books offer hundreds of techniques for developing this practice, so much so that it can be overwhelming.

Asking yourself what you have learned today cuts through all the excess and noise you may experience on any particular day. This simple practice is an easy way to use your journal to become a better person.

Once you have determined what you have learned that day, ask yourself a follow-up question. If, for example, the significant learning experience involved a mistake, you can ask yourself: How could I have avoided this mistake? When working with the mistake, reconstruct the scene in your imagination by writing it in your journal, and then reconstruct the situation by writing corrections in the journal. We do this work during the EMDR session. Using your journal to think through and redo a situation primes the psyche for EMDR. Journaling and spending time with this event reduces the likelihood of repeating the mistake. When describing the scene in the journal, you should provide as much detail as possible. Write down how you felt, why, what was said, and what you saw. Write it out like a scene in a play.

Explore how often this kind of scene has happened to you in the past and ask yourself if it happened with other people or just with this one person. When journaling, you are to think like an investigator. You want to understand what happened, how it happened, and why it happened. The goal of journaling is to discover the true motivation behind each party's behavior. In other words, ask yourself: What is going on here and why?

Next, you must determine how to correct this problem and reduce the likelihood of it happening again. Ask yourself what you would have wanted to happen in the situation, and then write, in as much detail as possible, a description of the preferred scenario. This technique is called "reconstructing the narrative" in your imagination. This practice is a powerful way to learn and grow.

If you do not do this self-evaluation and reconstruction, you will make the same mistake again. It is essential to write and correct the scenario. Journaling keeps you aware of what you are doing during the day, what you want to do and what you want to avoid doing. Awareness is the key that frees you from repeating the same mistakes. Exploring these few questions can cause a significant improvement in all areas of your life.

One entry, usually made in the morning, sets the goal for the day. The day's purpose can also be entered into the journal before retiring at the end of the day. Then review it in the morning before leaving the house. You might choose a spiritual goal, like trying not to do or say anything that will cause harm to another person, or you might want to attempt to be a better listener to those that come to speak with you during the day. You may want to examine your relationship with alcohol, unhealthy foods, or your devices and how you can better manage these relationships. A spiritual way to reach the day's goal may be to increase your time in silence with your journal.

You can change anything you want about yourself, but these changes should start with a journal entry followed by an evaluation of the effort at the end of the day. Assess your progress, examine the goal, and adjust. Use the journal to correct the problem.

Some of my clients say they think about the day's events each night before retiring, but they do not write the events down in a journal. Instead, they worry about family, relationship, or vocational issues that have plagued them for years, then play the scene or problem repeatedly in their head, imagining the worst-case scenario or feeling bad about themselves.

This habit of simply ruminating causes anxiety or depression, which disrupts mood, appetite, and sleep, and they are in an unhealthy place before long. These problems are manageable, but rumination causes them to become overwhelming and destructive.

I have counseled college students who thought their life and future was over because they received a *C* in a class. This single grade became an untamable monster. It caused a loss of confidence and ballooned into an imagined catastrophe of being unable to graduate, never finding a job, and not being able to find a wife or husband. Eventually, the vision of their future was that of a street person in some city. All this because of a *C* in chemistry or history. I still am amazed at the power of negative thoughts and the destructive and paralyzing grip these thoughts can have on us. EMDR is a gift because it dismantles this negative thinking in short order.

Suppose you reconstruct and correct the problem in your journal, combined with EMDR therapy. In that case, you will put worry and rumination to rest because you are seeking a solution and inevitably making progress to eliminate the problem.

You can see that an end is in sight because your actions will bring a resolution to the problem. You are no longer taking the victim's role but rather the hero's perspective. Problems often emerge in our lives. These are worldly issues. When attempting to solve a problem, you must use a problem-solving model. This book talks about the inner world and encourages behaviors and techniques that are the opposite of the outer world, but not when we are solving a worldly problem. The journal is an excellent adjunct to EMDR transformation, especially in stage four, chaos and confusion. It is this period of creative introversion where the client must find out what the next chapter of their life is going to be. During this period in our transformational work, a journal is a powerful tool.

PRACTICAL WAYS TO ACHIEVE EXCELLENCE IN YOUR CRAFT OF EMDR

We have discussed the adventure inward—a request to slow down and try to understand what is happening within you. There are two simple suggestions that I have to improve your therapeutic skills. I do not know how you improve your craft without doing this. You must videotape your session, not all of them but at least three or four a month. I do not expect you to record your entire week and watch it, just a few sessions to catch your mistakes or see your genius appear. Without this habit, you will not know if you are doing good work or not. It would help if you did this whether you are seeing a consultant or not. Second, seek consultation, preferably not from someone who has been using EMDR as long as you have been using it. I know the seasoned and older consultants might cost more, but it is worth it. People often ask me how I grew my private practice. They expect some marketing strategies or suggestions, but I say, "Excellence in your skills is very attractive to people."

Most clinicians want to get better at their craft; they travel around the country to train and learn new things. These efforts are necessary, but if you learn a new technique but do not know when to use it strategically, this new knowledge can harm the process of EMDR and the client. Learn everything you can, videotape yourself, and in that videotaped session, I hope you are in front of your client and you are able to forget everything you know and just wait, watch, and listen.

CHAPTER 15
DREAM AMPLIFICATION AND INTERPRETATION
AN ANCIENT SKILL FOR THE POST-MODERN AGE

The quote below is from Morton Kelsey, a Jungian analyst and writer. He tells us the value of dreams:

From some deep center of reality, a dreamer within speaks to us. This reality knows everything about us, has wisdom greater than ours, and provides these nightly dramas for our transformation. These dramas tell us who we are, where we have been, where we have strayed from the path, how we can get back on the path and where our destiny would lead us. (Kelsey, 1986, xxxv in Bosco).[1]

I have adapted Kelsey's description of the value of dreams and applied it to EMDR therapy so you can see just how compatible both activities are with each other.

From some deep center of reality, EMDR therapy activates our voice within to speak to us. This EMDR reality knows everything about us, accesses wisdom greater than ours, and provides access to our life's dramas for our understanding and eventually for our potential transformation. This EMDR process tells us who we are, where we have been, where we have strayed from the path, how we can get back on the path and where our destiny would lead us (Kelsey, adapted by Dobo).

So let us begin our journey into the dreams in the context of EMDR therapy.

DREAM THEMES WITHIN THE SIX STAGES OF TRANSFORMATION

Before we begin to discuss how to work with dreams, it is essential to know that during EMDR therapy, the dream themes are consistent and predictable across the course of treatment. This consistency and predictability make dream work for the EMDR therapist easier than you might think. We know that transformational EMDR consists of six stages. The next important thing to understand about dreams is they reflect where the client is in the therapeutic process. Dreams and even nightmares symbolically represent the stage the client is in at the moment the dream occurs.

Stage One: Avoidance Dream Themes

If they are in stage one, *avoidance,* they will have dreams with the theme of running away and hiding because something is chasing after them. It is the classic "I'm trying to get away, but I can only run in slow motion" dream. Sometimes they get injured but are not harmed because they are protected in some way. This type of plot may seem like a favorable dream, but it means the client is avoiding their issue. The new self cannot emerge unless the old self dies. Being indestructible in a dream is not good. It means your defensive mechanisms are still intact. You cannot have a resurrection without a crucifixion.

Stages Two and Three: Dream Themes of Surrender and Dismantling

These two go together because we are in destruction mode once you surrender. These dreams occur early in the therapeutic process. Sometimes they occur after the first EMDR session. These are often nightmares. These dreams are about death and destruction, storms, houses burning down, people dying. We are destroying the old cognition—the old self. These dreams will reflect this destruction process. Sometimes there are nightmares in this stage. It is essential to tell the client they might have vivid dreams or nightmares but to not be alarmed by them because they are temporary. If you do not warn them and they have a frightening nightmare sometimes, they will refuse to continue with EMDR, but if you tell them about the nightmares, you normalize the nightmare. The client is not alarmed because you warned them that this might happen. Warning them about potential nightmares does two things. First, if they have a nightmare, they think you are a genius for predicting it; therefore, you must know what you are talking about. Second, if they do not have a nightmare, that's fine. It's a win-win by giving them a heads-up about the possibility of a nightmare.

Stage Four: Dream Themes of Chaos and Confusion, Loss of Identity Stage

During this period of therapy, the client's dreams are about being lost, and they do not know what town they are in; they do not know how they got there or where they are going. If they do know where they are going, they do not know how to get there. They might not know how to get back home, to school, or anywhere familiar. Sometimes they do not even remember their name. They do not remember where their car is or how to find it now that it's lost. The dreams reflect the client's sense of being in a state of chaos and confusion, and loss of identity.

Stage Five: Dream Themes of Rebirth

The rebirth dreams are optimistic. There are children or baby animals in these dreams. The clients are learning how to be an *I do matter* person, so they are like children learning how to walk. Sometimes some women are pregnant. This symbol is not because they are having a baby (although it might be if they are pregnant). This theme of being pregnant symbolizes the rebirth they are going through at this stage. These dreams occur toward the end of stage four—the client dreams of being in a winter scene but can see a tropical island in the distance. People dream of Christmas, even if they are atheists, because Christmas is the beginning of the new way, the new hope.

Stage Six: Dream Themes of Assimilation

These dreams are inhabiting the promised land, dreams of fulfillment, although not entirely because the journey is never really over. Circles and squares are symbols of wholeness. The number four is what Jung describes as the quaternity. It represents many things, but an essential meaning is wholeness. I am sixty-seven and have been doing this work my entire life. After my son died, I recorded a series of nine dreams. A few of these dreams represent wholeness.

I doubt I could have survived my son's death without the foundation of my inner work. In one dream, I was cooking four eggs in a round pan. The chef grading us on our cooking said I cooked mine perfectly. I was able to eat the eggs. So the round pan and the circle also represent wholeness. Four is the number of wholeness. Eating is rare. The act of eating in a dream means something is being assimilated from the unconscious to consciousness. The fact that there are four eggs—well, eggs might be the beginning of life. These eggs did not get to live as chickens. They are dead and eaten—assimilated. One could say the same about my son. He had a life but did not get to live it. This is a very good dream for the dreamer but also sad. Jung said the inner dreamer is not moral but was right. The inner dreamer does not make the news; it just reports it. It is the last dream in the nine-dream sequence. I am probably accepting that my son is dead. EMDR significantly accelerated the grieving process for me.

Dream work is like other lifelong artistic endeavors; one lifetime is not enough. Fortunately, in this six-stage transformational EMDR process, the dreams seem to follow consistent themes in each stage; therefore, it is much easier to understand them. Morton Kelsey gives us three rules that I have followed my entire life in my dream work.

THREE IMPORTANT RULES AS WE BEGIN

1. *Write the dream down.* It is essential to bring the dream out of the mysterious world of the unconscious and into the three-dimensional world of time and space. You need to have a dream to interpret. Writing them down is the only way you will remember them. It is the only way you can ponder and work with them.

Bring them into the three-dimensional world, not the two-dimensional world of your cellphone or iPad. Write it with pen and paper. We have discussed the seriousness of creating a journal. Dream work should be approached similarly.[2]

2. *Take your dreams seriously* and spend time trying to understand them. As you read this chapter, you will develop skills that will make it easier to understand your dreams. In fact, it will make it exciting and fulfilling to spend time in this endeavor. In doing so, you will discover just how meaningful and serious this work is for you (Kelsey, 1978, 46).

3. *Write the dream in a journal, not on a device.* I will discuss the documenting of the dream in more detail later and make some suggestions in this regard later in this chapter. Even if you scribbled a few words in the middle of the night, you usually will remember the entire dream. If you don't write it down, you will almost always forget it minutes after waking up to begin your day. I am opposed to using devices for this work, but I am sure most of you keep you phone next to you at night and will make a note on it in the middle of the night instead of a notebook. If this is how you choose to recall a dream at night, that's fine, but when working with it, I encourage you to use a journal and pen of your choosing to work with it in the three-dimensional world of pen and paper.

People say "I do not dream" or "I do not remember my dream." If the inner dreamer provides important dreams only to have them ignored, it will stop providing a memory of them. If you can get a good night's sleep and go into REM, you dream. As you read this chapter, you will see just how much time it takes to examine a dream comprehensively. You will have a sense of accomplishment as you begin to understand this new language. You will also understand yourself in ways that you would never have imagined.

THE STRUCTURAL CHARACTERISTICS OF THE DREAM

Dreams usually have a consistent three-part structure, but not always. We might think of this three-part structure as the vessel in which the contents of the dream live. This structure is the skeleton of the dream. You might find this hard to believe because most people just say, "Dreams are weird." However, this lack of understanding is because most people do not try to understand their dreams. This situation is a sad state of affairs because dreams are not weird; dreams are brilliant, mysterious, and a fantastic resource throughout life. The dream's truth and wisdom are there for the taking. Dreams have a definite beginning, a middle, and an end, although these things are not always immediately apparent.

Carl Jung believed that dreams are a force of nature, a natural phenomenon. Dreams are not moral. The dream does not care if you die in the dream or live. It just shows you the truth. Nothing is more natural than something with a beginning, a middle, and an end. Our lives can be seen in three stages. Sex has three stages—beginning; middle, when intensity increases; and resolution. Literature and music have forms that are in three stages. The Catholic Mass has three parts. You do not have to look hard to see this natural three-stage phenomenon; it is everywhere.

Most dreams can be understood in a three-stage structure. You need to be able to identify each stage as you examine the dream. Learning to identify each of these three stages is your first task in this process of dream analysis. We must first examine the

dream for its three-part structure. After these three parts are identified, we will explore the anatomy of the dream. This is a more
detailed examination of the dream's content.

THE THREE-PART STRUCTURE

Part I: The introduction or the exposition. "The scene
opens." The exposition consists of two things: the scene or
setting and the characters. The characters are not always
human; often they are animals or unearthly beings. You
will be surprised how often the first sentence of a documented dream sets the scene as if the curtain has just gone
up and the actors are there to deliver their first lines. Do
not overthink this. Trust that the dream has a beginning,
and it is the first sentence or two of the dream you
recorded and decided to examine.[3]

Part II: The conflict or problem. This middle section is
where all the action happens. The plot is revealed,
tensions build, and the story begins to play out. Jungians
call it the *peripeteia,* that is, a sudden reversal of fortune.
The drama begins often with building tensions as the
story develops (von Franz, 1988, 43).

Part III: The resolution. This is the *lysis,* that is, a gradual
decline of tensions. It can resolve itself, or it can lead to
calamity. The dream can also end without resolution. It is
not the unconscious that creates the end of the story.
Remember, the inner dreamer reports the news; it does
not create it. It simply expresses what is going on in the
dreamer's life. The dream does not lie. It is not capable of

deceit. If you want to know the truth about yourself, begin to attend to your dreams. When you divide the dream into these three parts, you do not make any commentary. Use the exact words from the dream that you recorded and divide those words into three sections (von Franz, 1988, 43).

In summary, as you examine a documented dream, almost without exception, the first sentence or two reveal the exposition; the proverbial curtain rises. You immediately have the setting and the main characters. Then something starts to happen—the conflict or tension of the story plays out. Finally, there is the resolution or lack of resolution. These are the three parts of the dream's structure.

Let's examine a dream and break it down into these three structural sections.

THE DREAM

A man has two boys fishing at a lake.

An older man comes by and asks, "Why are you fishing here? Don't you know there are no fish in this lake; it's a dead sea."

The man responds, "These boys like to come out here to fish. They don't care if they don't catch anything."

The old man asks, "What are those two cells, those cages on the shore there?"

He answers, "That's where these boys live."

"Why do you keep them captive in cages?"

"I don't keep them captive. The cell door is never locked. They can leave any time they want, but they choose to stay here and fish in this dead sea." A reversal of fortune. An unexpected twist of fate. The dream ends.

IDENTIFYING THE THREE STAGES OF THE DREAM

What part of the dream is the exposition?

A man has two boys fishing at a lake. (Scene and characters)

What is the problem/tension/conflict?

An old man comes by questioning and informing them. "Why are you fishing here? Don't you know there are no fish in this lake; it's a dead sea."

The man responds, "These boys like to come out here to fish. They don't care if they don't catch anything."

The old man asks, "What are those two cells, those cages on the shore there?"

He answers, "That's where these boys live."

"Why do you keep them captive in cages?" (Plot—story unfolds)

What is the resolution?

"I don't keep them captive; the cell door is never locked. They can leave any time they want to, but they choose to stay here and fish in this dead sea."

EXPLORING THE CONTENT OR ANATOMY OF THE DREAM

Now that we understand the three-part structure of a dream, let's explore the contents of the dream. The contents give the dream life. Just like a human has a skeletal structure and organs that make the person a living thing, well, the same is true with dreams. The anatomy of the dream is its content. It's what gives the dream life. Just like the body has many organs, so dreams have many elements to examine and understand. The list of components is below:

The Anatomy of the Dream (The Components)

1. Symbols
2. Signs
3. Images
4. Metaphors
5. Emotions
6. Thoughts
7. Themes
8. Motifs
9. Fantasies

Not all dreams will have all these components, but these are the parts that your unconscious has available to deliver its message to you, the dreamer. You can read several different books about dreams, and this list might look different. I am not saying this is the end-all of dream content, but it has worked for me for decades. The first step is to understand each component. To do that, it is important to be able to understand what each component means and what each component might look like in a dream.

DREAM COMPONENTS DEFINED WITH EXAMPLES

A symbol: A symbol is an expression for something unknown. It represents something other than itself. It is more than itself. It may be familiar; however, it has more meaning than the obvious.

For example, we are all familiar with a cow. We know what a cow is and does. Most of us do not think of it as anything but an animal that gives milk and is a food source or an animal we see grazing in a pasture.

In India, the practice of Hinduism teaches that the cow is sacred. It represents one of the central tenets of Hinduism: Do no harm to an animal. If someone of the Hindu faith dreams about a cow, it will have a much deeper meaning for them than if an American of a different religion dreamed of a cow. For Americans, the bald eagle is a proud symbol of strength and patriotism, but it is just a bird for other countries.

A symbol is, on the surface, something with which we are familiar, but it has a hidden meaning of something more than meets the eye. Archetypal symbols are common to all people, and they are potent symbols, such as a serpent, cross, sword, and blood, etc. If you were to look any of these symbols up in a symbol dictionary, there would be pages and pages of what they could mean. This universal nature that is not limited to time or space is why the archetypal symbol is so powerful. The symbol generalizes throughout all of history. We will discuss these powerful symbols later in this chapter.

Signs: A sign is often related to a symbol. The difference between a sign and a symbol depends on the dreamer's perspective. A person might dream of a STOP sign as they drive along in a dream. The sign's meaning can simply be to stop as the dreamer drives along in this dream, or it may be symbolically perceived if there is something in their life that they are doing or about to do that is dangerous. Then this sign is much more important. The dream usually understands the STOP sign as something more significant than just a sign; in this case, it is a symbol. When something is a sign, it is less important than a symbol. A sign does not have multiple meanings for the dreamer; it has a more personal meaning, whereas a symbol has another meaning other than itself.

Fantasies: Fantasies usually occur while awake. Fantasies are like daydreaming. Jung developed a strategy employing an active fantasy he called active imagination. In this fantasy, the dreamer would reenter the dream while awake but calm and quiet with their eyes closed. The person is actively engaged to better understand the fantasy. In this situation, the dreamer can ask characters in the dream anything they want to ask. If the dream does not seem finished, they can continue it to its end. A passive fantasy might happen as you drive along on a long road trip. Passive fantasies can be valuable, too, especially if they contain dreamlike material. One has to be aware that these imaginational experiences are valuable. Einstein said, "Imagination is more powerful than knowledge." In my EMDR work, I have found this to be true. If these passive fantasies are ignored, they become like the inner dreamer who takes away the memory of the dream because the dreams are being ignored.

Sometimes the fantasy can be the inner singer. If a song pops into your head for no apparent reason and you're not sure why, it is a good idea to pay close attention to the words because they are almost always relevant to something going on in your life. When a client is processing during an EMDR session and says they hear a song, I want to know what song and some of the words. It is ALWAYS relevant to the work that we are doing.

Here is an example of one of my experiences with my inner singer.

I was away on an internship at Florida State University. The first week was team-building and getting to know everyone. One of the activities was to go canoeing with the other interns on a river. There were visible alligators around and lots of other interesting wildlife. I was a bit angry about being away from my family for this non-work week to go canoeing with the team. I was going to spend fifty-two weeks with these people. I felt that fifty-two weeks away from my family was quite enough. I didn't feel like I needed a fifty-third week. I could have spent another week at home with my kids and my wife. My boys were young at the time. My internship was going to be a year, and it was required to earn my doctorate.

As we were out on that river, an old, obscure song by Robert Lamm, the keyboard player from Chicago, popped into my head. The song was from his first solo album in 1975 that not too many people know. I had not listened to it in decades. My inner singer was reflecting my reality on that river with these words from this song, called "Crazy Way To Spend a Year."[4]

Remember, my internship was beginning and lasted exactly *one year*.

> *What am I doing here?*
> *Soaking up the atmosphere.*
> *Furthering my career.*
> *Crazy way to spend a year.*

Is this the perfect song for that moment on that river in a canoe, soaking up the atmosphere? Is it crazy for me to be canoeing on a river with alligators to earn a psychology degree? Furthering my career. The internship lasted precisely one year— crazy way to spend a year.

The unconscious is brilliant, and to ignore it is squandering perhaps the most powerful ally you will ever have in your life. It reveals the truth to you in dramatic ways and sometimes with a sense of humor. When you are working with a client and they report a song playing in their head, ask about the song. It is another way the unconscious communicates to assist with the self-healing power of EMDR.

Image: Images are the language of the dream. Dreams are nothing but images. Pay close attention to dreams that reoccur or change in some way. For example, vehicles are commonly understood to be our ego and how we navigate the world. If you are in a car but someone else is driving, you are most likely not in control of your life. Someone else is. Someone else is driving you. Sometimes you might drive but go too fast and lose control and crash. You are most likely moving too fast in an area of your life. Images are the language of the dream; notice which ones capture your interest.

Theme: Themes consist of a few words that concisely describe the dream. The theme captures its cognitive essence. The EMDR therapist sees the dream and wants to identify what negative cognition is present in the dream. Can you capture the negative cognition the dream represents? For example, is it a scary dream? Are you being chased by something dangerous? The theme might be *I'm in danger,* a negative cognition. Identifying the cognitive essence is how transformational EMDR therapists begin to integrate an understanding of the dream, first, by identifying the negative cognition that is present in the dream.

The second thing to consider is, does this theme fall into one of the six stages in our transformational model? The dream of the dead sea and the two boys fishing represents a client in stage four: loss of identity, chaos, and confusion. The boys are fishing in a dead sea— the sea of the poisonous king. There are no fish. They are afraid to leave their cells even though the doors are not locked. "They can leave at any time but prefer to stay." These factors tell us that the dreamer is in limbo, in the middle. He does not want to stay but he is afraid to leave—a lose-lose. The client realizes they cannot stay where they are in their life, but they do not know what to do to change. The adaptive shift to stage five has not occurred. The client is on the fence about making the necessary changes in their life.

UNION/TENSION OF OPPOSITES

This dead sea dream represents the idea of the tension of opposites, which is a core tenet of Jungian psychology. The tension is greatest when we experience joy and distress simultaneously. For example, my father died a few months before I earned my doctorate degree. Earning the degree was a great accomplishment, but I was also sad that my father was not there to see it. I had a dream where I was at a cemetery celebrating a birthday. This dream represents the union of opposites I was experiencing. Part of my life had died, my father. I was fatherless as I gave birth to a new life; a new profession was ahead of me.

Jung thought that a non-rational union of opposites was at work in all individuals throughout the life span. An encounter with the opposites enables the individual to ultimately overcome their conflicts by accessing what Jung calls the transcendent function. This is evident in EMDR, where the *I don't matter* conflicts with *I do matter*. EMDR resolves this conflict by accessing the client's inner transcendent self, and thus the conflict between these two ways to see the world is resolved. It is the conflict between the allegiance to the poisonous king and a move toward the sacred king.

Let's examine the union of the opposites in our dream.

1. The boys were free yet captive.
2. They stayed in their cell, but the door was opened.
3. They were free but not free.

4. They were fishing but not really because there were no fish. Fishing in a lake with no fish.

Other common themes: Often dream themes can be identified by an emotion or a negative cognition. People often dream of being in school for an important test they forget to prepare for. The dream theme might be *I did something wrong, I'm to blame, I'm stupid,* or *I'm in trouble.* These are also common EMDR cognitions, as is this anxiety dream.

People have falling dreams. The unconscious is trying to wake up the dreamer with a bang. This falling dream could be in some of the early stages of our transformational model. If you avoid it, you might get one of these falling-to-earth dreams. If you are the dreamer afraid to make a move, stuck in a jail where the doors are open, you are free to leave but stay. You might end up with this falling dream.

Dreams of being killed: Remember, we discussed the necessity of dying in a dream so the new self can be born. Dying is not always bad in a dream. The EMDR cognition might be *I'm in danger, I'm going to die,* or *I'm not in control.* The method of death and where the fatal wound occurs in the body are also telling. Beheaded, shot in the heart, shot in the back, throat cut. These methods of dying in dreams are metaphors for what is going on in the person's life. If the client is stabbed in the back, they might have been betrayed. If their throat is cut, the client does not have a voice. If a client is beheaded, they might be out of control in some areas of their life: "I'm losing my head." So the theme for us is to see if a negative cognition is present in the dream and then ask what stage this dream represents. An entire book could be written about dream themes, but fortunately, during EMDR therapy, there are only four themes to be concerned with during the transformational EMDR process.

The themes we discussed earlier are avoidant dream themes, where the client is running away or protected so they cannot die. No one can get to the dreamer, like the bulletproof vest dreamer we discussed earlier. If the dreamer is unwilling to die, he cannot be reborn. The dismantling of the old-self dream themes, which are filled with death and destruction content, can be nightmares because, as you will recall, we are in destruction mode in therapy. Dreams of chaos, confusion, and loss of identity have the client not knowing who they are or where they are going in the dream. Sometimes they are stuck in the middle of something. One of my clients dreamed he was on a broken-down raft in a storm. He knew he was halfway across the sea. It would take just as much effort to go back as to go forward. He decided to go forward in the dream and in his life.

The rebirth and assimilation dreams are our last theme. They are more optimistic dreams where children or newborn animals are often in the dream—symbols of rebirth like Christmas or Easter. Even atheists have these symbolic dreams that represent the rebirth they are experiencing.

Emotions that the dream creates are usually self-explanatory, but it is helpful to identify the feeling if it is not mentioned in the dream. The dead sea dream might conjure a feeling of helplessness or confusion even though no emotion is mentioned. This dream is lifeless, just like the characters in it. The scary dream is easy. That would be fear. The dream of not being prepared for the test might be anxiety and fear. Emotions can sometimes guide you to a thought about the dream or yourself. The anxiety from not being prepared might suggest themes like "I'm a failure," "I'm in trouble," "I'm stupid," etc. The emotion of fear because you are chased might be, "I'm in danger" or "I'm not in control."

Motif usually relates to a symbol. For example, the boys are fishing in a lake. The motif is that there are not fish. The symbol of the lake has a motif of being dead, a dead sea. Jung describes a motif as it relates to the symbol of a tree. The motif of the tree will describe whether it is growing, is dead or bears fruit. Basically, the motif tells us a little more information about the symbol. For example, in the dead sea dream, the motif might be the boys are free and not free or that the sea has no fish; it is a dead sea. These components are examples of motifs to the symbol.

These components make up the basic anatomy of the dream in addition to the structure that provides the settings and characters, along with the story, the conflict, and finally the resolution of the story.

Experiential identifier: It is good to ask the dreamer what their overall experience of the dream feels like for them. It can have a theme that is one of our negative cognitions accompanied by an emotion. Most important dreams have an emotional component to them. If we understand that Phase Three of EMDR therapy is our procedural steps, also known as the assessment phase, we have built this phase's essence. There are three primary components to the procedural steps. First, we need to establish the troubling image, which we call the target. Second is the negative cognition that pairs with the target image and finally the emotions the client experiences when thinking about the target and the thought is our third core component. Dreams are images, so we ask the client to isolate the most upsetting part of the dream, which is our target. We have seen how to develop a negative cognition from the dream, and finally, we have the emotional experience the dreams create. These three elements are the essence of the procedural steps: Target. Emotions. Negative Cognition. A way to remember this is by using the acronym T.E.N.

Types of dreams: It is essential to be aware of the types of dreams that occur during the transformational EMDR work. This list is not exhaustive; these are the most common dreams that occur during EMDR therapy. There are three types of dreams we will discuss. They are personal dreams, archetypal dreams, and precognitive dreams.

Jung would call specific dreams *Big Dreams*. These dreams are archetypal ones that utilize archetypal images and are usually remembered throughout life. These dreams are often remembered without writing them down. As the person ages and develops, the "big" dream has a different meaning. This same dream can mean one thing in your twenties and then have a deeper meaning in your thirties and yet a completely different meaning in your sixties. The archetypal dream has many meanings, often simultaneously. Such dreams often leave the dreamer with a numinous experience as if they have been touched by God or the universe, something bigger than themselves.

WHAT ARE ARCHETYPAL DREAMS AND SYMBOLS?

A working definition of an archetype is the original pattern or model from which all things of the same kind are copied or on which they are based; a model or first form; prototype. In Jungian psychology, it is a collectively inherited unconscious idea, pattern of thought, image, etc., universally present in individual psyches. If you look at any dictionary of symbols, many of the objects you find are archetypal.

For example, a serpent or snake, a sword, water, blood, or specific numbers four, three, and eight. Geometric figures circle and square. The hero, villain, colors, planets, etc. Archetypal symbols transcend culture, time, and space. Common archetypal themes include war, lust or sex, death and destruction, greed, and the seasons. A holy quest is an archetypal journey. The hero's journey is archetypal. The transformational work we are discussing in this book is an archetypal journey. Each person is a hero in their own quest to find their true self and true purpose.

Personal dreams are dreams that deal with events of the day. The car is often symbolic of our ego, which we use to get around in the world. However, if you are a car mechanic, you may dream about a car in a more personal and less symbolic way. Just as if you are a banker or financial advisor and dream of money, that may mean something more personal than if someone who was not in the financial business was dreaming of money.

Finally, occasionally there are precognitive dreams. These are dreams that coincide with a future event. The dreamer might dream that someone they love died in a car crash. Usually, this does not mean the loved one will be in a car crash. More often, the dream is about you crashing somewhere in your life, and the characteristics you might possess, like this loved one in a dream, hint at where your crash is occurring. But sometimes, the loved one has a car accident, and the dream predicted it. Again, this is rare. If it does happen, first, it might be a coincidence. Second, beware: One can have an inflated sense of self if they believe they can foretell the future. Third, some people do have precognitive dreams.

The chronological age of the dreamer is important to consider. Younger people are directed to the world. They are making their place in it. They have a strong link to material things and the outer world. Older people begin to withdraw, as they have already made their place in it. It is a more sublime look inward and coming to terms with what is next—reconciling with God.

We have already established a dream's three-part structure below:

1. What is the exposition?

A man has two boys at a lake fishing. The scene and characters are revealed.

2. What is the problem/tension/conflict?
There are no fish. They seem to be prisoners who are free
to go but choose to stay in this empty existence. Tension of
opposites, free and caged simultaneously—that is tension
although not obvious.

3. What is the resolution?
They remain in this situation of fishing in a dead sea with
no fish. There is no resolution; it is a dream of waiting.

What are the symbols?

Fishing
Dead sea water (with no fish)
Caged but free
All men in the dream
Old man
Two
Boys

What are the emotions this dreamer might be feeling? Helpless, stuck, confused

What are some ideas about the theme? The first theme that
comes to mind is the boys are stuck, unable to go even though
nothing and no one is stopping them from leaving. This dreamer
might think of a theme from the negative cognition perspective: I
can't trust my judgment. (I don't know if I should stay or go.)
They might feel like they are doing something wrong. Someone

will be upset if they change their life, so that might be a theme. You can see how important it is to have the dreamer's input. We can make all sorts of guesses, but it is really the dreamers who will know.

What is the image? The sea and shore. Seeing the cages. Seeing little boys fishing. The image might seem like the man is a caring father, but he is a prison keeper. He is not a father but is a father in the image. He is not a captor but is sort of a captor. Opposites.

What is the motif? The boys are free but not free. They choose to stay. They don't mind not catching anything. The lake often symbolizes the unconscious. A lot is happening below the surface, but not in this dream. The sea is dead, which would be a motif related to the lake. Cages are usually locked to hold captives, but these are not locked, a motif related to the cages.

With the structure of the dream identified and the components of the dream examined, let's explore the mechanics of dream interpretation. It is best to sit quietly and let your mind contemplate the symbol. You can do this with a pen and notebook in your lap. It is okay to write while you contemplate. Sit quietly. This practice is not meditation. It is just an attempt to stop the distractions of the day. Just a few minutes to quiet the noise in your head and try to recall the dream. You are the one who has the answer to the mystery within.

The first example below demonstrates the correct way to amplify a symbol and is an excellent place to start. The second step is shown in the following diagram, the incorrect way to amplify and work with a symbol. You do not have to make a diagram. You can just make a list of ideas. You can write the ideas in a journal in paragraph form. This work is in the service of your journey, so document it in any way you prefer.

You may associate more with a symbol than the five in the example. The diagrams are just to demonstrate the right and the wrong way to begin the amplification process: the more associations, the better. You must always return to the symbol for an association. Each of the five associations is generated by the stimulus "fishing." Fish-water/fish-productive/fish-apostle/fish-food/fish-fufilling.

The Proper Way To Amplify a Symbol

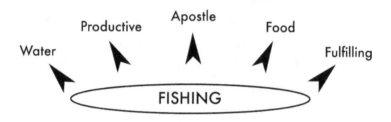

The example below describes how *not* to amplify a symbol. In this example, the symbol creates an association, food, which is correct. Then, however, the next association is not from fishing.

In this example, food is the stimulus word associated with pizza. Do not generate an association from an association. Always return to the original dream symbol for the subsequent association. Do not do this: Fishing-food-pizza-Italy-spaghetti-Grandma Marie (makes the best spaghetti).

You can see how ridiculous it can get by chaining an association of an association to an association. Next, you'll be at grandma's, who makes the best ravioli. Never generate your association from an association because it will take you into the abyss and entirely in the wrong direction. Always go back to the symbol as the stimulus for the association. Of course, there may be genuine associations to relevant associations, but they will be related to the original symbol too.

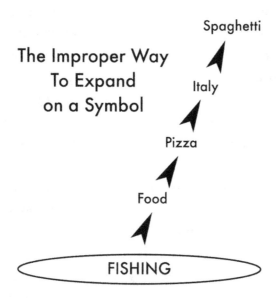

Let's examine a dream from the structural perspective and then examine its content. In other words, let's do a comprehensive exam and give our interpretation. Read the entire dream from beginning to end once.

Let's take a look at a new dream and put our new dream interpretation skills to work. First, identify the structure. Remember it is divided into three parts. As a reminder, here they are:

Exposition—the curtain opens to the scene and characters appear.
Conflict—the ups and downs of the dreams.

Resolution—sometimes it is resolved, sometimes unre-solved. Often there is a twist of fate, a reversal of fortune.

As I examine the dream for the first time, I note anything that interests me as I take the first read through the dream. I am not so concerned about whether something is a symbol, sign, or image at this first read-through. I'm just moving through it once to see what I notice before breaking it into the three structural parts.

One important thing to remember to ask yourself frequently is why the unconscious chose that symbol and not something else. For example, a woman had a dream where her father injured her right thigh with a circular saw. The saw cut her thigh while she was in the shower. The unconscious could have chosen any number, weapons, or method of injuring the woman. It chose a circular saw. Why did it choose a circular saw? You look at this symbol from multiple points of view. There are many ways to wound a leg, so why not a sword or a knife? Why a circular saw? Within the symbol "a circular saw" is the word circular. What does circular mean? Round and round it goes; where it stops, nobody knows, as the saying goes. When asked why a circular saw, she knew precisely why it was a circular saw. We will examine her understanding of the circular saw symbol later.

OUR NEW DREAM

1. The initial read-through of the dream should be exactly as the dreamer wrote it. There is no concern for grammar at all. This is symbolic work, not logic work.

I was walking along through a luscious green meadow when I reached the edge of a cliff, I was with someone, but this person didn't seem to be doing much for me, they were with me but without interaction. I don't know who it was but had a feeling it was a known person. As I looked over the edge of the cliff, I could see fledging birds, I became very fearful for one, I really liked this young bird and it was desperate to fledge but cautious, I was also very scared for this bird because at the bottom of the cliff was a massive river which flowed around the earth at high speed, like a raging torrent. I had a sense that it could take me anywhere I wanted to go but I was afraid of this river, and I didn't want the bird to fall in, I started to climb down the cliff to protect the bird, all the time worrying about the water.

Step One: Divide the Dream Into Three Structural Sections
Italics are phrases that caught my attention during the first read-though.

Part 1: The Exposition: The scene opens, exposing the setting and the characters.
I was walking along through *a luscious green meadow when I reached the edge of a cliff* (opposites—meadow and cliff). I was with someone, but this person didn't seem to be doing much for me, they were with me but without interaction. *I don't know who it was but had a feeling it was a known person.* (Knowing and not knowing/with me but not with me; Jung said the soul/psyche speaks in sense and nonsense. That sounds like nonsense to me or the struggle in uniting opposites, a common Jungian struggle.)

Part 2: The Plot: The story unfolds.
As I looked over the edge of the cliff, I could *see fledging birds*, I became very *fearful* for one in particular, *I really liked this young bird* and it was desperate to fledge but cautious, *I was also very*

scared for this bird because at the bottom of *the cliff was a massive river which flowed around the earth at high speed, like a raging torrent.*

Part 3: The Resolution: Lysis

I had a sense that it could take me anywhere I wanted to go *but I was afraid of this river* and I didn't want the bird to fall in, *I started to climb down the cliff to protect the bird*, all the time (being afraid and yet brave enough to climb down) worrying about the water. THE END

Whenever anyone talks to me about their dreams, almost without exception they say, "I had a dream last night, and it was so weird." I hope this example demonstrates just how normal dreams are when looked at as a story with a beginning, middle and an end. A story with characters, structure and robust content components.

Let's examine the content with our new amplification skills.

Symbols and their associations

- *Idyllic luscious green meadow:* safe, calm, peaceful, soft, gentle, relaxing, stagnant, lulled to sleep by the peacefulness, boring
- *Cliff:* dangerous, exciting, fear, high, hard, rocks, jagged, awesome view from on high, opportunity
- *Birds:* helpless, vulnerable, fly, wings, soar, die, fall, free as a bird
- *Raging river:* dangerous, valuable, helpful, treacherous, fast, eternal, cold, deep, fast, fun

Images

The image of the lush green meadow; the view from the cliff and looking into the raging river; the view of the fledging birds on the cliff; the mysterious companion with no name, face or gender.

Emotions

- *Confused:* I know the person I'm with and didn't know the person; he/she did not do much to help me. Apathy.
- *Dilemma uncertain*: If I retreat to the meadow, I might be lulled to sleep, bored, unfulfilled. If I climb down to the river, I could die or drown.
- *Fear* for the birds and of the cliff and the river. Concern climbing down to protect the birds. *Bravery:* climbed down to help despite fear of the situation.

Themes

An adventure genre: I can go anywhere, but it's dangerous. The archetypal quest. The call—will it be answered or not?

Motifs

"I like the young bird." "Fledgling birds." Knowing and not knowing the person who accompanied her.

INTERPRETATION FROM OUR ASSOCIATIONS

Symbolic Interpretation:

Water often represents the unconscious, but a river, different than a lake or sea, also appears when someone is in transition. A river flows from destination to destination. It is important to stay above the water on a boat safely in this raging river. Jump in and you can be consumed by the unconscious unless you are very aware of what is going on in yourself—a strong swimmer, as it were.

The raging river: The dreamer can ride the river anywhere she wants to go. There are two ways to move, by air and water as she stands on the earth, to get where she is going. There is freedom above and below, but she is stuck in the middle on the ground. The river can take her anywhere, but it's dangerous. You are free to go anywhere—but the journey might kill you. She has birds that can't fly and a raging river without a boat.

The fledgling birds is a phrase used more than once by this dreamer so it is important. It mutes what birds often symbolize. A bird often symbolizes freedom and accomplishment. Birds can soar high. I feel free as a bird. However, these birds in our dream can't fly, let alone soar. The good news is that she will protect and keep the fledging birds safe so they can grow and fly.

In stage five, people often dream of children and small, helpless animals. These symbols reflect the rebirth that is slowly occurring. "You have to be as little children to enter the kingdom."

In stage four, people often want to retreat to the old way—the safety of the lush meadow.

Opportunity is stalled by fear or just caution. Opposites: lush meadow, cliff. Birds and sky above, river below. The river moves fast. Climbing down slow and carefully. A person with me I know and don't know.

Emotional interpretation:

Confused (I know *the* person I'm with and didn't know the person): He/she did not do much to help me. Apathy. Indifference.

Dilemma uncertain: If I retreat to the meadow, I might be lulled to sleep, bored and unfulfilled. If I climb down to the river, I could die or drown—fear for the birds and of the cliff and the river.
Concern: climbing down to protect the birds.
Bravery: climbed down to help despite fear of the situation.

What is the inner dreamer trying to reflect to the dreamer?

This person apparently is going through significant positive changes in her life. There are obviously challenges because change, although necessary, is often riddled with struggles to get to the other side of the transformation.

What stage is this dream from in the transformational stages?

In stage four, with a solid move to five. The bird is a component of stage five, the rebirth. The danger of retreating to the meadow is the seductiveness of retreating to stage three and not completing the journey. She did not retreat, but the option was there. Instead, she left the lush meadow with no mention of it ever again. Her focus was on everything in front of her, not behind her. That is an excellent sign. Remember, dreams do not lie. She is indeed moving forward in her transition. There was no hint of a retreat.

THE CONCISE INTERPRETATION

It is time to leave the safety of the lush green meadow, the safe zone. She never looked back and only was moving forward carefully. She is moving toward a new adventure, although dangerous, that would take her anywhere she wanted to go.

The young bird is the dreamer, and the woman in the dream is also the dreamer. She is not sure she can manage the cliff. Part of the dreamer is like a newborn bird unable to fly yet, still a brave adult woman who can navigate the dangerous cliff without falling into the river below. These are skills the baby bird does not possess. She reflects courage, climbing to protect the little bird despite her fear of the cliff and river. The protective adult self can care for the younger emerging childlike self, and together, using the adult's wisdom, can bring the young self safely off the cliff. She must wait a while to find a way to get onto the river. The vehicle will take her anywhere she wants to go on earth. Or she can care for the bird until it is time for it to fly high and soar free —yes, free as a bird. We don't know the end of the story yet.

I HOPE after learning these new skills for working with dreams you can see how interesting they are. Do you not want to know what happens next with our dreamer? Does she retreat to the meadow and play it safe, or does she find a way to navigate the river courageously, getting to her true destination? Or does she nurture the youngest bird to adulthood so it can soar and fly *as free as a bird?* Or does she crash like Icarus, who got too close to the sun by being reckless? We do not know. The suspense is as intense as a TV drama where you must wait until next week to see what is going to happen.

My editor once said, "Dreams are boring to read. Andy, if you want to put your reader to sleep, put a dream in the book." If, however, you are armed with an understanding of the dream, asking yourself, "Where is the exposition; where does the plot begin; how will this end?" as you read you immediately identify the important symbols and see the dream's images in your mind's eye, all while you start to feel what it would be like to be in this dream. Then the theme of the dream comes into focus. With this new understanding, you have turned a sleepy dream that will put a reader to sleep into something that creates great curiosity within. It is as if there is a great mystery and you are gathering evidence, using newly acquired forensic tools to unlock the meaning. Sherlock Holmes is afoot—alert, skilled and curious.

Yes, reading a dream can put the uninitiated to sleep, but armed with the three-part structure, you will now immediately look for the exposition, the middle conflict, and the resolution or lack thereof. You will start to spot a symbol, image, and other phrases and feelings that jump off the written page. You now are armed with skills to look at a dream, much like a surgeon looks at an X-ray. All the while you will be thinking of where you want to begin to amplify the contents of the dream. Sleepy is not what you will now experience. Now you will be like Sherlock Holmes investigating the mystery of the dream.

While others say, "I had a dream; it was so weird," you will know there is nothing weird about it. In fact, it is clear as day, and at times, the unlocking is like magic.

THE DANGER OF USING UNQUALIFIED SOURCES

I once picked up a dream book from some new age author. I opened it to a random page. Surprisingly, it opened to a dream about being pregnant, a common theme in EMDR transformational work, so this was something I knew a great deal about. The author said it was likely that the dreamer was going to have a baby. WHAT! That's it? That statement just shows how completely ignorant the author was of dreams, the unconscious, and the power of symbols. This author did not even think for a second that being pregnant could be a symbol or a metaphor related to something going on in the person's life. Many people in the transformational stages four and five have pregnancy dreams.

These are great dreams and offer encouragement to these clients who have fought hard to get this rebirth dream. Distilling these wonderful dreams to something so wrong is damaging to the dreamer reading a book written by someone who is totally unqualified to be tampering with material of the unconscious.

In my work, as I have said, clients often have pregnancy dreams. In the dreams, sometimes they are assisting in the pregnancy or with the delivery and sometimes they are pregnant. These clients are men and women in their fifties, sixties and seventies. They are not going to have a baby. Sometimes men have such dreams, and I doubt they are going to get pregnant in their life. Call me crazy, but I think that is a safe bet. If a woman is pregnant, of course, pregnancy dreams are common. It is wrong to interpret and present a dream in just one way. In this particular book, the symbol was pregnancy, and the interpretation was this one thing: You're pregnant in real life, end of story. Also, do not use one of those gazillion ridiculous dreams-interpreted books by unqualified charlatans, please. The work is serious. Use serious resources.

SYMBOL DICTIONARIES

There are many excellent dictionaries of symbols that are far more helpful than books that interpret dreams for you. It is not the dream you want to understand as much as the symbols the inner dreamer is offering you—one should work to understand the language of symbols and not simply seek information. When I find a used-books store, there is usually a reference section where old, wonderful dictionaries of symbols sell for just a few dollars. I have quite a collection. To get started, here are a few of my favorites:

A Dictionary of Symbols by J.E. Cirlot
The Penguin Dictionary of Symbols
The Book of Symbols: Reflections on Archetypal Images

Studying and reading books by Jungian writers is a safe bet, as their therapy model is based on dream work and over a hundred years of research. Their knowledge, I find, is vast and based on science, observation, and experience.

If you do not remember anything else from this book, remember this: Symbols are eternal and, therefore, not limited to one meaning. Nor is the dream limited to one period of a person's life. A woman who had a pregnancy dream while carrying a child may recall that dream thirty years later and understand a new meaning of being pregnant as an aging woman psychologically or symbolically rather than literally.

As stated earlier, Jung's "Big" dreams are usually filled with archetypal eternal symbols. These dreams become relevant at different stages of a person's life. Big dreams are much like our personal myths. You can read a myth and enjoy the story when you are ten or twelve years old. But in your twenties, perhaps studying the story at a university, you understand there is a deeper meaning to this story as one gets into adulthood. Then in old age, one can even have a deeper understanding because you may have lived that myth.

In high school, our class published a literary magazine called *Icarus*. I did not know what a literary magazine was then, but I did know about Icarus. I just thought it was one of those stories I had to study in English class. Now, fifty years later, my son, who was flying too close to the sun, died in August 2022. As I wrote earlier, I, like Daedalus, warned him. I told him more than once, "If you don't slow down, you will die before you are forty."

Like Icarus, he ignored the warning of the father. He came

crashing to the ground. That story I read in high school has a much deeper and more accurate meaning in my life today. As a high school student, I identified with Icarus disobeying his father. Now, as a father who lost his son, I am Daedalus, crushed by the death of the son who did not heed the father's warning. To say myths are just stories and dreams are unimportant misses the richness of life. The story of Icarus is comforting in a way. It reminds me that no one is protected from tragedy or death. We always think it won't happen to us—the overused cliché. And here I am, the father of a dead kid who was consumed by work and his incredible success. He just did not know how to slow that train down.

Let's examine our circular-saw dream.

This is shared by a friend who read my first book and offered this for this book.

A CLOSER EXAMINATION OF THE CIRCULAR SAW DREAM

> I was in the shower, trying to get ready for some event, and my father came into the bathroom nude and got in the shower with me, rubbing his body on me and trying to rape me. The really odd (in my opinion) part is that he had a circular saw with him and used it to cut my right thigh while we struggled. The image of my thigh being cut by the saw—the skin kind of crunching away (if that makes any sense)—I'll never forget that image.

In real life, she was emotionally abused by her father, not sexually, and her father physically abused her brother. She was, however, sexually abused by someone she did not know.

Exposition: I was in the shower getting ready for some event and my nude father came into the shower with me.

Plot: He was rubbing his body on me and trying to rape me. The really odd part is that he had a circular saw with him and used it to cut my right thigh while we struggled. The image of my thigh being cut by the saw—the skin kind of crunching away.

Resolution: I'll never forget that image (thigh being sawed).

CONTENT

Symbols: shower, water, circular saw, right (leg), father

Associations: shower—*Psycho* movie; shower clean; shower steam; water; sexual; naked; vulnerable; usually relaxing. Circular saw—round, loud, bloody, violent, cut off above the knee, electric, round and round again and again. Wound of the right leg.

Emotions: scared, angry, frightened, trapped.

Thoughts: I'm trapped, not this again, what is he doing, I have to get out of here.

Theme: assault and violated; vulnerable.

Images: bloody loud attack in the shower.

Metaphors: circular saw, going round and round, right leg might mean being right.

THE CONCISE INTERPRETATION

The interpretation is an exchange with me and the dreamer as we both work to understand the dream's meaning as it relates to her work during EMDR and her life. This dreamer said that her father would emotionally abuse her and physically abuse her brother over and over as kids, a never-ending cycle. Hence the circular saw. She stated that she recently severed ties with her parents, which was difficult. The dream was telling her she was RIGHT. The circular saw was cutting her "right" leg off. Dad violently tried to deny her truth. Wounds in the legs often refer to being stuck at a standstill in one's life.

She stated that she was indeed at a standstill in her life. She stated:

"I remember thinking that I had to get out, and it was almost an 'oh no, not this again' kind of feeling. I felt scared, angry, and trapped. The severing of ties with my parents and the cutting of the leg could be related to that 'being stuck.' I had this dream before I decided to sever ties. But yes, I'm at a standstill with the sexual abuse I only recently discovered I experienced as a baby. I did move forward but am at a standstill in that area.

"I haven't had sex in over a year, and my marriage is suffering. Seeing something recurring and having no way out resonates with the emotional, verbal, and physical abuse (against my brother, me, and any pets we owned)."

Circular (saw), your unconscious, could have used any number of symbols to injure the leg. It chose the circular saw for a reason. Circular is essential, as is saw. Saw could be "You *saw* something happen," not the cutting of your leg in the dream, but you saw something that was RIGHT—the truth—and someone is trying to cut it away. This thing you SAW may be an endless reoccurring thing, like round and round and no way out. Circular.

Themes: Dad is not dad. Dad is a perpetrator. I'm in danger. I'm trapped. I'm going to die.

Use the dream interpretation worksheet and try one of your own dreams. You can also download these worksheets from my website at EMDReducators.com.

DREAM INTERPRETATIONS WORKSHEET

Exposition:

Plot:

Resolution:

Anatomy/Contents: *Remember all dreams do not contain all of these components.*

Symbols:

Signs:

Images:

Metaphors:

Motifs:

Themes:

Emotions:

Thoughts:

Fantasies:

From the analysis of the content, write your concise interpretation.

CREATING AN EMDR SESSION FROM A DREAM

Incorporating our dream interpretation skills with the standard EMDR protocol is not difficult. EMDR is an image-friendly therapy. The target is always an image. Dreams are nothing but images, so this is an easy thing to do.

The purpose is to take the dreamer into the dream again. C.G. Jung developed this imaginational technique that he called active imagination. Jungians take the dream of their clients and ask them to go back into the dream. They do this by sitting calmly, relaxing, trying to get into a meditative state. Once relaxed, they recall the dream and ask a question to characters in the dream as they continue the dream. Some of these experiences can be long and detailed, and sometimes they last only a few minutes with new insight.

The work is accelerated significantly by using the active imagination strategy and combining it with the bilateral stimulation of EMDR. It is like Jung's active imagination strategies on steroids.

Now let's use the material from our "fledgling bird" dream interpretations and complete the standard protocol of EMDR. We usually begin by asking the client what the most distressing moment in the dream was. She chose to climb onto the cliff to protect the birds. We then explore the theme of the dream that provides the negative cognition. She identified two possibilities, *I can't do it*, or *I am weak*, as her negative cognitions. When we start the stimulation, she will have to decide on the most robust one when she thinks of the target. The completed protocol is below.

Target: Climbing on the cliff to protect the bird
NC: I can't do it or I'm weak—we settled on I'm weak
PC: I can do it or I'm strong
VOC: 3

Emotion: scared, terrified, determined

SUDS: 7

Body: heart is speeding up

So, you see, a dream is a natural experience. It often is accompanied by images, thoughts, feelings, and body sensations. Dreams integrate very quickly with the standard EMDR work.

THE JOURNEY NEVER ENDS

Finally, as the therapist, much of this book was about you being the companion to the hero, but eventually, you as the therapist must sit in the hero's seat and find a companion for your own transforming hero's journey. Also, you should know that journey never really ends. I am sixty-seven years old, and I have been invited yet again to accept my reality, to accept the changes the world has thrown me. My friend and colleague said she has a reframe when bad things happen: "This is not happening to you; it is happening for you." As much as I hate to admit it, that is true, at least for me. I leave you with a wondrous experience that happened a few days ago related to the loss of my son and best friend of sixty-two years.

While writing this book, several synchronistic events happen to me. When one is in a life transition, they occur more frequently. Some I shared here, and some I kept to myself. Today, I am going through the final changes to this manuscript, putting the final touches on it, but somewhere in the universe, the message says, "Not so fast." Ryan, from the first line in this book, is going to close this book out.

Ryan called me a few days ago and said he had a dream he wanted to share with me. I am always interested in anyone's dream. When trainees share a dream, I usually record the video on zoom, which I did with this dream of Ryan's. One thing I did not mention in the chapter about dreams was that sometimes your client will have a dream for you and you for them.

In my first book, I talk about the Saint Elizabeth dream that literally changed how I understand the human psyche. My client hated God. She was an atheist because her father, a big man in the church, physically, sexually, and emotionally abused her. She had no idea who Saint Elizabeth was, but I did, and this dream was relevant to both of us.

Ryan was reluctant to share his dream with me. He said he prayed about it and talked to the dream's characters. "Should I share this with Dr. Dobo?" In these meditative explorations, the answer he received from his transcendent inner self was, "Just tell him." So he told me.

He said he had read my blog the day of the dream called "Death Bed EMDR." The blog describes the first and only session of EMDR I did with my dear friend John, who was in hospice, and also about the death of my son John. Both of my two Johns died within twenty-four hours of each other. I also described my inner rage.

Ryan said the blog affected him deeply. Ryan went to sleep and stated that in the middle of the night, he started to feel like he had a fever and was congested and started to sneeze. This sneezing is something he said had never happened to him before. He thought he was getting sick and would probably be unable to work in the morning. Out of consideration for his wife, he went to the couch to not wake her. He immediately fell asleep, and as soon as his head hit the pillow, he started to dream. He said this dream was very different. "It felt weird," different than any other dream he had in the past because it felt so real. Here's the dream.

Ryan is telling me this. He says:

Dr. Dobo, you and I are in a restaurant; it is one of my favorite restaurants in the world. It is in Savannah, and it's called *Jazz*. I took my wife there for our anniversary. It has excellent food, and there are always jazz musicians playing old-style jazz with an upright bass player and a singer singing Billie Holiday stuff. It's a fantastic place. So in this dream, you and I are playing together. You are playing piano, and I am singing into an old-school microphone, but we are doing an Abbott and Costello routine, making everyone laugh. Then suddenly, you slowly break into a beautiful song on the piano, and the entire room stops laughing, and the whole crowd gets very quiet and listens to the piano. Everyone is mesmerized by this beautiful song—even me. Everyone is totally keyed into what you're playing, and after you do the final run on the piano and the song ends, you say, "And that, ladies and gentlemen, I call that song, 'The Two Johns.'" Then I say to you, "Both Johns got baptized." Then you hit the piano, chuckle, and shoot me a wry smile, and the dream ended.

After Ryan told me about this dream, I could not speak. I was overcome with emotion as my eyes welled up with tears. I was far too angry about these two deaths so that I could not have this dream, so Ryan had it for me, and his dream brought me more comfort than one could ever imagine. The two Johns are okay. It is comforting that my friend John, whom I met when we were both five, is with my son, which is very reassuring. I am so glad dreams have been part of my life since I was an undergraduate. I do not know how I would have gotten through so many troubled times without their reassuring voice.

I hope you, who are EMDR therapists, will begin your inner journey if you have not already begun that work. I hope this book has opened you up to the idea that there is more going on in

EMDR therapy than reducing symptoms and discharging your clients. I hope you come to understand the importance of myth in our work and also in our life. Michael Meade tells us that myth means emerging truth. The truth about ourselves, our clients, and the world. You may not see the myth in your work, but it is right there in front of your eyes. You only need to knock, and that door will be open to you. The choice is yours.

Like I always say, EMDR is a lightning bolt of transformational power, but if you do not know how to access it, then EMDR is reduced to the power of a flashlight battery. Good luck on your EMDR journey.

ACKNOWLEDGMENTS

There are many people to thank as I complete the final words in this manuscript. Some writers map out their work. I do not. I just start and try to see where the writing will take me. This is probably not the most efficient way to write, but it's my way, for better or worse. When I began this project, I could share my ideas with my good friend John Whalen, who was a professional editor in his youth. We have been friends since kindergarten. We shared just about everything over the years. Before I finished this book, John died the last day of July, and less than twenty-four hours after John died, my younger son, also named John, died unexpectedly and tragically. I mention this because both men would have read a portion of this manuscript and offered valuable feedback had they been alive at its completion. So I wanted to acknowledge them posthumously.

My wife, JoAnne, has always supported me for my entire life. None of these things matter if she is not by my side. She has read these pages more times than I care to say. She is a kind but critical voice. This has been a challenging year. One cannot survive things like losing a child without a deep and endless love. We have been blessed to have such love for each other since we were just kids. Within the tragedy, we are lucky. Jung's union of opposites strikes again.

I want to thank my brother Rob, who has supported me in any harebrained idea I ever had, from the time I played in bands when he would always come out and listen, to opening a video store in the '80s and reading and promoting my books back home in Pennsylvania. I can always count on his support.

I want to thank Ryan Terry, LMHC, and Melissa Fernandez, LMHC, who permitted me to share some of our work together. Their youthful excitement about this work keeps this old man young and excited too. I also want to thank Dr. Cori Calkins, who read portions of this manuscript in its first incarnation and provided excellent feedback. I also want to thank Gwen Forbes-Wolfe, LMHC, for her keen proofreading eye.

As I continue to train therapists, I have great colleagues that help and support me: Jackie Flynn, LMHC; Dr. Pamela Rinato; Sandra Stanford, LMHC; and Rotem Brayer, LPC. They have always supported my work, and I support theirs. I am so blessed to have such seasoned, mature, and skilled experts to help me train new therapists in EMDR therapy.

I would like to thank my patients and trainees. I work hard to teach and help them, but they also teach and help me every day. This work is not a one-sided process. It is an exchange. A soul-to-soul exchange. Hopefully we both benefit from our time together.

I would also like to thank my education coordinator, although she is much more than that. She is a caring friend who tolerates and understands my forgetfulness and carelessness. I tell folks that Theresa is my frontal lobe; this is not an exaggeration. Having her support has added years onto my career.

I would also like to thank Chris Kridler, who is one of the smartest and most talented people I have ever met. She wore many hats on this project. She is my sometimes videographer and video editor, my book editor, cover designer, and everything else required to get this book ready for the presses. Without her, this book would have never made it to print.

I want to thank the writers who enormously influenced my

worldview, Morton T. Kelsey, John Sanford, and Robert A. Johnson, whose books I continue to read and reread. These Jungian writers were the making of me. Francine Shapiro, for the enormous contribution she has made to the world in the service of reducing human suffering. Also, Laurie Beth Jones, whose book *The Path* provided a navigational tool for me when I was a young man lost. A book I recommend to my clients who take on this Hero's Journey. And much later in my life, I was fortunate enough to have her as a business coach as I began to move into my new role as a mentor and trainer to other therapists.

I would like to thank my older son Andrew, who this book is dedicated to. There was no one closer to my son John than his brother, Andrew. When they were toddlers, we called them Chip and Dale. They just always had so much to say to each other. That never changed. He has handled the loss of his brother with the strength of a true hero, which by the way includes a river of tears, because we therapists know there is a time to cry, and in those times we must cry.

Finally, I'd like to thank you, the reader. If you got this far, then I hope you have a new perspective of the work. I hope you will invite the pattern of the hero into your thinking. I hope you will understand and begin to use Transformational EMDR. This untapped power of EMDR changes everything and sets the hero's journey in motion. Good luck on your journey.

NOTES

1. ACCESSING MYTH

1. Castaneda, C. (1972). *The Teachings of Don Juan: A Yaqui Way of Knowledge.* Berkeley, CA: University of California Press, 20.
2. Hari, J. (2021). *Stolen Focus.* New York, NY: Random House, 10.
3. Jung, C. G., & Shamdasani, S. (2012). *The Red Book Liber Novus.* New York, NY: W.W. Norton, 236.
4. Meade, M. (2016). *The Genius Myth.* Seattle, WA: Greenfire Press, 56.

2. SETTING THE STAGE FOR THE HERO'S JOURNEY

1. Sanford, J.A. (1977). *Healing and Wholeness.* New York, NY: Paulist Press, 93.
2. Johnson, R. T. (1998). *Balancing Heaven and Earth.* New York, NY: Harper Collins, xi-xii.
3. Metheny, P. (2018). *Speech at Society of Neuroscience.* San Francisco: Society of Neuroscience.
4. Csikszentmihalyi, M. (1990). *Flow: The Psychology of Optimal Experience.* New York, NY: Harper Collins Publishers, 11-14.
5. Bukowski, C. (2016). *Essential Bukowski.* New York, NY: Harper Collins, 48-50.

3. TRANSFORMATIONAL STAGE ONE: AVOIDANCE

1. Wilson, E.O. (2017). *The Origins of Creativity.* New York, NY: Liveright Publishing Corporation, 165.
2. Dobo, A.J. (2018). *Unburdening Souls at the Speed of Thought: Psychology, Christianity and the Transformational Power of EMDR.* Sebastian, FL: Soul Psych Publishers, 69.
3. Johnson, S. (2005). *Becoming an Emotionally Focused Couples Therapist: The Workbook (1st Edition).* New York, NY: Routledge, 67.
4. Campbell, J. (1972). *The Hero with a Thousand Faces.* Princeton, NJ: Bolling Press.
5. Bly, R. (1990). *Iron John.* New York, NY: Addison Wesley Publishing Company,

209.

6.　Johnson, R.A. (1974). *He: Understanding Masculine Psychology*. New York, NY: Perennial Publishing, 8.

7.　Bukowski, C. (2016). "Roll the Dice." In *Essential Bukowski*. New York: Harper-Collins Publishers, 210-11.

8.　Sanford, J. (1993). *Mystical Christianity: A Psychology Commentary of the Gospel of John*. New York, NY: The Crossroad Publishing Company, 257.

9.　Bly, R. (1988). A *Little Book on the Human Shadow*. San Francisco, CA: Harper Collins, 48.

4. THE ADVENTURE BEGINS

1.　Jones, L.B. (1996). *The Path*. New York, NY: Hyperion, 49-92.

2.　Eliot, T.S. (1943). *Four Quartets*. New York, NY: Harcourt Brace Jovanovich, *59*.

3.　Bukowski, C. (1967). Tales of Ordinary Madness. San Francisco: City Lights Books, 195.

5. SELF-HEALING

1.　Shapiro, F. (2018). *Eye Movement Desensitization and Reprocessing Therapy: Basic Principles, Protocols, and Procedures (3rd Edition)*. New York, NY: Guilford Press, 28.

2.　Jung, C.G. (1961). *Memories, Dreams, Reflections*. New York, NY: Random House, 170.

6. SIX STAGES OF TRANSFORMATION

1.　Shapiro, F. (2002). *EMDR as an Integrative Psychotherapy Approach*. Washington, DC: American Psychological Association (Edited by Shapiro), 46.

2.　Edinger, E.F. (1993). *Anatomy of the Psyche*. Peru, IL: Open Court Publishing Company, 1.

3.　Leeds, A. (2016). *A Guide to the Standard EMDR Therapy Protocols for Clinicians, Supervisors, and Consultants*. New York, NY: Springer Publishing Company, 4.

4.　Jung, C.G. (1970). *Collected Works, Volume 14: Mysterium Conjunctions (second edition)*. Princeton, NJ: Princeton University Press, § 2.

5.　Jung, C. G. (1960). *Collected Works Volume 3: The Psychogenesis of Mental Disease*, Princeton, NJ: Princeton University Press, § 396.

7. AVOIDANCE

1. Dobo, A. J. (2018). *Unburdening Souls at the Speed of Thought: Psychology, Christianity, and the Transforming Power of EMDR*, Sebastian, FL: Soul Psych Publishers, 67.
2. Chodorow, J. (1997), *Encountering Jung: Jung on Active Imagination*. Princeton, NJ: Princeton University Press, 14.
3. Hillman, J. (1989). *The Blue Fire*. New York, NY: Harper Perennial, 18.

8. SURRENDER

1. Dobo, A.J. (2018). EMDR Training Manual. Unpublished, 79.
2. Jung, C.G. (2012), & Shamdasani, S., *The Red Book Liber Novus*. New York, NY: W.W. Norton, 236b.
3. White, V. (1983). *God and the Unconscious*. Dallas, TX: Spring Publications, 164.

10. CHAOS AND CONFUSION

1. Source: https://quotepark.com/quotes/820331-cg-jung-the-highest-most-decisive-experience-is-to-be-alone

12. THE JUNGIAN LEXICON

1. Jung, C.G. (1971). *Collected Works Volume 6: Psychological Types*, Princeton, NJ: Princeton University Press, § 279.

13. FINDING YOUR PLACE OF POWER

1. Bukowski, C. (2016). "Roll the Dice." In *Essential Bukowski*. New York: HarperCollins Publishers, 210-11.
2. Phillips, R.E. III, & Pargament, K.I. (2002). *The sanctification of dreams: Prevalence and implications. Dreaming, 12*(3), 141–153.

15. DREAM AMPLIFICATION AND INTERPRETATION

1. Brown, E.M. (1986). *Dreams, Visions and Prophecies of Don Bosco.* Hawthorne, CA: Don Bosco Publishing, xxxv.
2. Kelsey, M.T. (1978). *Dreams: A Way to Listen to God.* New York, NY: Paulist Press, 44-45.
3. von Franz, M. (1988). *The Way of the Dream.* Toronto, CA: Windrose Films Production, 43.
4. Lamm, R. (1974). *Crazy Way to Spend a Year.* Los Angeles, CA: Lamminations Productions, 3.

UNBURDENING SOULS AT THE SPEED OF THOUGHT: PSYCHOLOGY, CHRISTIANITY, AND THE TRANSFORMING POWER OF EMDR

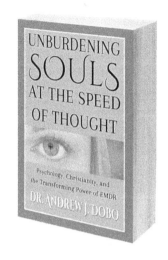

Unburdening Souls at the Speed of Thought: Psychology, Christianity, and the Transforming Power of EMDR is about the transformative journey to wholeness that was modeled by Christ and is accelerated by a ground-breaking therapy known as EMDR (Eye Movement Desensitization and Reprocessing).

You will see an emotionally scarred surfer recover from the ultimate loss, the tragic death of his son. You will learn how dreams and images gave subjects the courage to change careers and enrich their lives. And you will discover how a woman accessed a buried traumatic memory during a therapy session and gained an enduring sense of peace.

The process described in psychologist Dr. Andrew J. Dobo's book occurs in six stages, which are mirrored by six moments Christ modeled in his Passion. Psychology and religion collide in the book's incredible tales, which move from despair to hope, hate to love, and fear to contentment.

This is a book that will give hope to those suffering mental anguish as they are exposed to a new map of the soul modeled by Christ and shared by psychology. It shows how survivors of trauma can heal and overcome negative beliefs about themselves. It's for those who want to better understand the workings of the soul and for those who do not even imagine such a thing exists. And it will fascinate any reader interested in the power of the mind.

About the Author

Dr. Andrew Dobo was first trained in EMDR in 1998 while in graduate school. He has administered over 15,000 EMDR sessions in his career. Now his days are spent consulting, writing, and teaching other therapists about EMDR therapy.

Dr. Dobo is highly credentialed in EMDR and has lived his life as a Jungian. He recorded his first dream in 1978 while studying music as a young man living in Chicago. He has never stopped using his dreams as navigational tools in his life. He eventually noticed that as he was using the EMDR model, he was also integrating Jungian thought, which included dreams to explain the EMDR process with his clients. This observation eventually gave rise to his books.

It became clear to him that EMDR activated a transformation

journey that the clients were invited to travel during his work with them. He noticed the clients moved through six stages and these six stages encompassed the twelve steps of a hero's journey identified by Joseph Campbell.

These observations were the catalyst for this book and his innovative EMDR trainings.

He hopes more therapists will see the value of myth that exists during EMDR. He invites every EMDR therapist to try and hold mythic space in our evidence-based model of EMDR therapy, because there is room for both to exist in the same space simultaneously.

You can connect with Dr. Dobo on social media.

Website: EMDReducators.com

[f] facebook.com/emdreducators
[in] linkedin.com/in/dr-andrew-j-dobo-36595673
[o] instagram.com/emdr_educators
[▶] youtube.com/drandrewdobo
[twitter] twitter.com/emdr_educators